THE SUCCESSFUL
Woman's MINDSET

THE SUCCESSFUL
Woman's MINDSET

UNLOCK THE SECRETS OF SUCCESS,
ACTIVATE YOUR POWER

GALIT VENTURA-ROZEN

Empowering University

THE SUCCESSFUL WOMAN'S MINDSET:

UNLOCK THE SECRETS OF SUCCESS, ACTIVATE YOUR POWER

By Galit Ventura-Rozen

Empowering University Publishing

ISBN-13 Print Edition: 978-1-7915042-1-2

ISBN-13 E-Book Edition: 978-1-7329994-1-1

CONTENTS

I met Galit when she was one of my clients, and through the Women of Global Change (WGC)–I have watched her soar ever since! She approached me to launch and open the WGC in Las Vegas and became President of the Las Vegas Chapter. Galit's dedication to service, community and women's empowerment was self-evident and she has now become the WGC National Chapter Director, which is no small accomplishment. I am thrilled to introduce a book that addresses my favorite subjects—women, business and success!

Galit's experience makes her the perfect person to write about the successful woman's mindset. It is a truism that successful people have a certain way of thinking and certain ways of doing things and that they develop certain habits that bring them to a life of success, and it all starts with our thought process. How we think affects how we feel, which then affects our attitude, which in turn affects our behavior, which finally affects our results. Our thoughts are also the birthplace of the desires that feed the flames of our energy, allowing us to tap into the well of action versus just reacting to the circumstances in our life. But the mindset is always the first step.

In her amazing book, Galit leads us on the ultimate journey of self-discovery and empowerment by sharing the secrets of the successful woman's mindset. She will open your mind to the possibilities and opportunities that lie before you and help you step out into the world with more confidence to embrace all of who you are. Each of us has a personal calling and a personal gift to bring to the world. Each one of us is different and as unique as our fingerprints, and yet we share many common elements, especially as women. But how is it that some women manage to run successful businesses and lead fulfilling family lives while others struggle, hearing their dreams like a faraway voice, beckoning them from some distant horizon?

This is where Galit and her book come in. In *The Successful Woman's Mindset*, Galit lays out tools and techniques specifically for women. It is well-known that women's minds work differently than men's. As women, we are natural entrepreneurs and natural multitaskers and we wear many hats–we are the daughters, sisters, friends, partners, mothers, and managers in both our households and careers.

Women have a natural inclination toward cooperation and collaboration. On a deep level, we know that where one woman succeeds, all women succeed. The business world has been male-dominated for many centuries but women have carved themselves a niche over the last 50 years or so and we are coming of age, so to speak. And as much as the patriarchal systems have served us, the time for balance has come. Indeed, the world is in need of women's leadership, female mentors and balance right now.

So how do we go about it? When we go into "work mode," what does it mean to go into it authentically as women, as feminine leaders? How do we learn to balance our business and personal lives? How do we move beyond the stereotypical models? The truth is that the more we learn, and especially from someone like Galit who is a living example of what she teaches about how to operate and incorporate our skills in both our careers and personal life, the easier this transition into leadership will be.

So, what would you do if you knew for certain that you could achieve your deepest purpose in life? What has your inner voice been longing for? The truth is, you are the one who holds the key to start living a more fulfilled life. A life with more satisfaction, fun, and fulfillment. A life of performance, energy, and engagement in all areas, of being authentically you and stepping into all you know you can be and all of who you are, with confidence and more clarity.

This book offers a unique opportunity to learn how to step into the required mindset to achieve the mindset of a successful twenty-first-century woman, which means stepping into your role of feminine leadership. Galit's book is a true gem; in it, she shares with you proven customized systems that will assist you from wherever you are in life and take you to higher levels, as well as practices that will free you of any limiting belief you might have, and into success. *The Successful Women's Mindset* will show you how to unlock the secrets of success, as simple as that!

Dame Shellie A. Hunt

Founder/CEO

www.SuccessisbyDesign.com

www.WomenofGlobalChange.com

From as far back as I can remember, I was always called "the girl who wears rose-colored glasses" and was known for seeing the world from a glass half-full perspective. There was even a period where I thought about writing a book called *Glass Half-Full*. What does all this have to do with how I came to write this book? As a self-professed optimist, one of the things that baffles my mind more than anything is the idea that these are my thoughts and if they're my thoughts, why can't I control them? All right, maybe "control" is not the right word, but why can't I change a thought every time one comes up that I would prefer not having?

Think about it. It's your brain. Why are there

times when your thoughts work against you instead of working for you? Wouldn't you think you would be your own cheerleader? Your biggest supporter? I think that's probably where *The Successful Woman's Mindset* came into existence for me. This mindset is associated with choosing to stop beating yourself up and instead changing the way you think and look at things. Changing your thoughts and making choices with your mindset that puts you on the path to success, through a growth mindset instead of a fixed mindset. I'll be sharing this in greater detail in the first chapters in this book. But in a nutshell, a growth mindset is knowing that you have the ability to be, do and succeed in everything and anything you want, whereas a fixed mindset is believing that what you have today and what you are today is limited.

A little over a year ago, before I started writing this book, I was asked to speak at the local National Association of Women Business Owners luncheon in Las Vegas. I started brainstorming and thinking of ideas and topics that would interest women.

With all the experience that I've had in over 25 years as an entrepreneur, starting at the age of

21, it was important to me to share *The Successful Woman's Mindset*. I can teach my executive clients the tools to be successful all day long through the experiences that I've had, what to do and what not to do to be successful. But if they don't have a growth mindset, it doesn't matter what I teach them. If their mindset isn't where it needs to be to wrap their head around those tools and be able to implement them in their businesses, professions and life to be successful, the tools are worthless.

I never saw myself as an author or even writing a book. Ever. Then, I realized it's my duty to pay it forward and share with you the things I have learned in over 25 years, in one shape or form. Why? So you can find it within your mindset to find the type of success you desire in your business and in your life.

ACKNOWLEDGMENTS

More than anything, I want to thank my three children, because they motivate me every day to be the best me I can be. So they can be whatever they choose, by knowing that if their mom can and has led the path to success, they can succeed even more.

I also want to thank my parents. I'm blessed to have the most wonderful parents. With every crazy idea I have had, such as returning to school when I was 38, leaving a lucrative career, starting over in a new business because I wanted to follow my passion and my purpose, they have supported me every step of the way, even when, at times, they may have thought that my decisions maybe weren't the best for me or most secure.

My mom is always there to love me, to tell me how amazing I am, and to love my children, and my father is always there to uplift me, mentor me, and tell me how much he believes in me.

I also want to thank the man in my life. He came into my life at a difficult time when I was going through some of the hardest times. He stood by me as my best friend and knew that we were supposed to be together, even though all I wanted was to be alone. He held my hair when I cried, held me when I needed it most and has supported me, telling me how wonderful I am and how much he loves me every day. Even through tough times, he stands by me because he sees in me what, at times, I don't see in myself.

Thank you to my brothers. I'm blessed to have three younger brothers and close relationships with them, their wives and children. To be such a close family that we can choose to work together, have dinner together, go on vacation together, I wouldn't have it any other way. Each of my brothers, in one way or another, has been there in support and has allowed me to be the big sister caring for them at times.

I have the most loving extended family with supportive cousins, aunts and uncles. I am thankful for my relationships with each of them across the globe.

This book is in memory of my grandparents that I have the most beautiful memories of always believing in me. They instilled in each of us the importance of supporting and loving each other, even if we are located all over the globe. I am blessed with a close-knit family and I'm thankful for everything I've learned, every experience we've shared, every vacation we have taken, growing up with a family that was so large and lovely. They showed me I would always have somebody there for me.

I want to thank my mentors. I have been blessed to have mentor after mentor in my life who have believed in me and seen where my path was supposed to take me, so that I can impact, influence and inspire as many people as I can to be what they are meant to be and to believe in themselves.

I would like to thank my best friend. We have gone through hell and back together and it's incredible to have a person in my life who knows me better than anyone, who will always be there for me through thick and thin and, more than anything, how different the two of us can be in every which way, but still be there for each other day and night.

I want to thank my numerous friends near and far. Some I have met, others I know from the online world. Thank you for your support, encouragement and some of the best cheerleaders around. Your friendships mean the world to me.

To my contributing editor. Thank you for your time and passion in getting across my words, in keeping my voice, and in making sure my thoughts came across to the reader the way I would like them to.

Last, but not least, I would like to thank **YOU**. The woman who inspires me every day to continue to share every last experience, challenge, and piece of knowledge. The woman who strives every day to be the best version of herself.

SHE HAS A GROWTH MINDSET

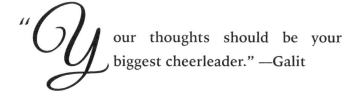

"Your thoughts should be your biggest cheerleader." —Galit

SUCCESSFUL WOMEN KNOW the growth mindset is imperative for happiness, fulfillment and success. It sets the guidelines for our initiating beliefs and attitudes and it results in effective action. A *growth mindset* is the belief that your thought process is for learning and expansion, and that you are not limited by what you know today.

When you wrap your head around the growth mindset, which is a large element of this book, you begin to understand there are no limitations to what you want. *You are your biggest limitation.*

I am a pretty sweet person. I can smile all day long and share with you the things you should improve. I am also told often that I can be tough, and I can be. I will always tell you how it is, and telling you that you are probably one of your greatest obstacles to having a growth mindset is just me being honest. There just is no other way that I will write this book. I wouldn't even know how to cookie-cutter it or sugarcoat it.

It is important for you to recognize that a lot of the attitudes and beliefs you have will only turn into effective action once you yourself recognize where they come from, why you have them, and how to get past them. That really is what a growth mindset is. Those limiting beliefs could have been imposed by family or friends, a significant other, or even our children. Maybe they just didn't give you the support that could have helped you develop more confidence, positivity and beliefs that you could be and do what you desire.

This book recognizes that may have happened, but doesn't spend a lot of time on it. Why? Because today is about you. This book is about you. *It's your turn*. If you're reading this book, it's possible you're ready to take action to remove those limited beliefs. You're ready to embrace *The Successful Woman's Mindset* characteristics and incorporate them into your daily life. You're ready to start seeing the domino effect that will happen when you embrace your growth mindset. The possibilities and the potential are endless.

What is the Mindset? It is the established set of attitudes that define what you believe about yourself and what you believe about your most basic qualities. Moreover, the Mindset is what can motivate you or stop you from what you want to achieve in your life. At its essence, it's your thoughts and how you think of yourself.

This statement boggles my mind most days and I know that when I figure out the answer to this next question, I will make sure to share it with the world.

"They are our thoughts, right? Then why can't you control them? Do you ever feel like your thoughts are your own worst enemy?" Now connect that to mindset.

One of the things that pushed me to go back to school and get my master's degree at the age of 38 was this actual question. While getting my master's in therapy, much time was focused on how to teach someone how to change their thoughts about themselves. I knew this was a valuable piece to help women be successful in anything they desire to accomplish in their lives.

Let's look at the Growth vs. Fixed Mindset. When I was preparing to give my first keynote on *The Successful Woman's Mindset,* I spent time researching studies on my theories. What I found was Carol Dweck, PhD, a psychologist and a pioneering researcher in the field of motivation. She looked at why people succeed (or don't) and how to foster success. With over 6 million views of her TEDx talk, you could say she is an expert in growth mindset vs. fixed mindset. I had never used this terminology before, but I knew there are people in this world who believe they can't and those who believe they can. It was Henry Ford who said, "If you believe you can or can't, you are right." I agree with that statement.

Fixed mindset. You believe your basic qualities. "This is how intelligent I am." "This is how talented I am." The extent of these qualities is fixed. "Nothing else can be taught to me." You spend time documenting instead of developing.

You worry about how adequate your talents and your intelligence are. You're always worried about proving yourself to somebody or something.

Growth mindset. You believe your basic qualities can be developed with dedication and hard work. It's just a starting point. Wherever you are today can be whatever you want it to be. You must find the tools, find a support system, or find a way to get there, but there's always a way. All successful people have a growth mindset. They know if there's something they want to accomplish, they don't always need to know how right away, they just need to believe they can.

Simply put, a fixed mindset is the belief that you are limited by your current knowledge. A growth mindset is the belief that you are not limited by the things you know today. The great part of understanding the fixed vs. growth mindset is knowing that this is all your perception of how things are at this exact moment.

For example: If today you have a high school education, you are 40 years old and working in what you consider a low-level job, and you believe you are stuck in this place for the rest of your life due to the limitations of your knowledge, experience and education, then you are living in a fixed mindset world.

However, if you understand that this is your position today but you can learn, gain knowledge and grow to apply for that dream job and change your life, then you are in a growth mindset world.

Seems simple, right? Then why do so many of us women **ALLOW** the fixed mindset to stop us? Instead of believing we can do more, we stop and settle. Why are some women open to challenges, overcoming obstacles, and finding a way to accomplish what they want, while many women are not? The answer to this question is **YOU**. You are the reason. We could look back at your upbringing, your limited beliefs from the environment you grew up in, we could look back at your teacher's, relationships, parents and so on.

We could spend an entire book just looking for the reasons many women have a fixed mindset. I do not believe in looking to the past for excuses. Yes, excuses, these are all excuses. I understand and sympathize with anyone that has a reason or multiple reasons to have a fixed mindset and I am sorry for the negative experiences you have lived. What if, instead of focusing on "this is why you are this way or that way" or why you aren't accomplishing the things that would be your definition of success, today you make a different CHOICE? Instead, today you acknowledge, "I have a fixed mindset and am ready to have a growth mindset!" Repeat after me: "I make the choice today to have a growth mindset!"

Now what? You're aware you have a fixed mindset. You're ready to be open to having a growth mindset. A mindset where you are ready to explore limitless possibilities and ways to grow, to have the things that you want in your life. It could be a job, a business, a relationship. There are many things that are out there for you once you make a choice, yes, a choice, to be open to having a growth mindset. Once you do, you will know the *how* exists. Once you figure out what you want to learn, and what you want to grow within yourself, the possibilities are endless.

If you already have a growth mindset, commend yourself. Let's keep it growing with *The Successful Woman's Mindset* characteristics.

2

SHE KNOWS HER DEFINITION OF SUCCESS

"*A* woman has the potential within her to succeed at everything she desires." —Galit

THE MEASURE of success is different for everyone. I do not believe in writing a book that tells you what success should mean to you or if you can consider yourself successful. Rather, in this chapter, you will learn quite a bit about the idea of "success by your definition." When I hold workshops to teach the blueprint of success, I start out with wanting to understand what success means and looks like *for you*. It could have many definitions, depending on the person.

I could compare two different women with completely different lives and they both could be considered equally successful. I believe each person has their own definition of success. If you don't know what that looks like or you don't know what that is right now, that's okay. There is a reason you picked up this book, there's something you're craving to learn, something you want more of for yourself in your life or your business. Keep at it until you learn what your own definition of success is.

The Webster dictionary's definition of success is: "The accomplishment of an aim or purpose." That is a short definition for a word that means so much and so many different things to different people. What does success mean to you? What does success look like to you? When I ask, the response I receive most is, "I don't know what success means to me." I teach the concept of success by your definition. It's okay if you don't know what your meaning of success is. The first place I recommend you start is to ask yourself, "Who is the last person I thought, 'That person is successful?'" What personality characteristics did that person have? What is it about their life you see as successful? There is nothing wrong with wanting to be like someone else. Just make sure that achieving what they have will make you happy and will make you feel that you, too, are successful.

We spend so much of our life comparing ourselves to others: the kind of families they have, the jobs they have, the money they have, the travel they take, and their relationships. We don't realize that spending all that time comparing ourselves to others and wanting what they want isn't really helping us toward our desire to have *The Successful Woman's Mindset* and to be successful in our life.

A lot of times when we talk about success, people immediately think about how much money they're making. We know there are many people out there making lots of money, but they are unhappy. Always think of success according to your own definition. Do not allow somebody else's definition to be yours, unless you agree.

When I started *The Successful Mindset* Series, I wanted to start with *The Successful Woman's Mindset* first. I didn't think to myself that this is a place to tell people how to be successful or to show people what success should mean to them. For me, what was most important was that every individual woman who read this book thought to herself, "Yes, I have had success in my life, and I want to continue having success in other parts of my life." "I really would love to be successful in my own right, in the way that I choose to be," or, "When I look at (insert name), I want to be like her." Therefore, it is more important to me that while you are defining your meaning of success, you go within and dig deep.

I get asked quite often, "What does it mean to go within?" Because if you're visual, you think to yourself, "How can I go within?" What it means is to take the time to close your eyes, to see the vision, to see what your life would look like at the moment that you believe you have *The Successful Woman's Mindset*, that you have achieved success in your life.

I often say I am a work in progress. But let me explain to you why. It's not that I think I'm not successful. It's that I want to continue to grow for the rest of my life. When I meet one level of success, I'm ready to go to the next. If you have seen any of my videos, read my book or know me at all, you would know that's because my success is based on the amount of people I have an impact on, the number of people I teach to recognize they can have the success they desire and want in their life.

That's why every time I meet one level of success, I set up a standard for the next level, and I can see myself doing that for the rest of my life. For you, you get to decide. You get to decide if meeting a level of success is enough. I don't decide for you, and please don't let somebody else decide for you.

Here is a quick activity, so you can work on defining your meaning of success. First, think about somebody you are familiar with, right now, that you may or may not know personally. Maybe read about in the news, read their books, follow them on social media, know from your community. Someone that when you see or hear about that person, or read about them, you immediately think, "Wow, that person is successful, I want to be like that person."

Maybe there are many things about that person you like or would love to embody. This is where you start figuring out your definition of success. Then, you dig even deeper. What is it about their personality? What is it about the things they've accomplished in their life? Is it building a family? Is it starting their own business? Is it a career? Are they impacting the world?

Write all of that out. Really focus. Now ask yourself, "What elements of this list am I missing in my life? What on this list, if I implemented or achieved, would add value to my life and make me feel I was successful?"

With my methods, you will learn how to take your definition of success and integrate the characteristics into your daily life to reach those goals and accomplishments that you desire.

There is nothing wrong with seeing someone else as successful. There is nothing wrong with taking those attributes that attract you to that person to help you to form your definition of success. You then would have the success you desire in your life.

With this book, I want you to find your own meaning of success. I want you to take the methods that I share in this book and learn from them, implement them, and know that you are the one that gets to decide how and when you meet the true successful woman's mindset.

3

SHE KNOWS OPRAH STATUS IS ACHIEVABLE

"*I*t doesn't matter who you are, where you come from. The ability to triumph begins with you-always." —**Oprah Winfrey**

YOU MIGHT START this book thinking to yourself, "How can I have *The Successful Woman's Mindset?* How can I be like Oprah?" or someone else that you see in the media, idolize, or look up to. What I have found interesting in speaking to many women is there really isn't that much of a difference between them and Oprah or somebody else they might find admirable. One of the main differences is associated with their mindset and not believing in themselves.

I remember when I was growing up, I was always a bit awkward. I had long legs, I was always taller than the other girls. I had a different name and a hoarse voice. My parents have accents. I remember many times I just felt like I kind of got lost. I got lost within *the norm*.

When you're little, you want, more than anything in the world, just to fit in. Yet I remember days where I just didn't feel like I did. So I would look up to either somebody I idolized on television, in the media, or even maybe another girl in my class that just seemed to be "normal." It's interesting because when we're younger, society and schools spend a lot of time trying to get us to fit in a box. As we get older, we learn more and more that fitting in a box is not the way that we become successful.

Then what makes you different from someone like Oprah? Look at her life. Look at her childhood. Many people know her story. She's gone through life-changing experiences many of us will never experience or can even fathom. Yet look at the success she has attained while giving back and having balance in her life. What makes her different from you? You are what makes her different from you. There's only one Oprah, and there's only one you.

When you choose to embrace your differences, your unique characteristics, you recognize you are perfectly you. Are you quirky, exciting, unique? At the end of the day, no matter what, there's only one you, just like there's only one Oprah, so why would you even try to be like Oprah?

Let's stop for a second and clarify this. I don't want you to be like Oprah. What I asked was, "What makes you different from her?" What I am trying to focus on is the element of success. What makes you believe you don't deserve the same success she has or more, or better yet, the kind of success you desire and want? If the success you want is like Oprah's, it can be yours. But it starts and ends with your mindset and believing in yourself. Look at all the things she experienced, and she found a way through it. How did she do that? Mindset. I believe she learned through her experiences how to have *The Successful Woman's Mindset*.

No, I don't know Oprah, and maybe I'm making some assumptions, but from watching the success she's had, the influence she's made on the world, the impact of almost everybody knowing who she is because of the great work she's done and continues to do, I believe that Oprah has *The Successful Woman's Mindset*.

If you choose to embrace this book and learn what it takes to have a Successful Woman's Mindset, who knows, if you want to be, you can be more successful than Oprah could have ever imagined. If that's not what you want, that's fine. This chapter is about the fact that many of us women, including myself at times, question, "What makes me so special?"

I spent most of my life trying to be normal and fit in. I can tell you from experience, I am anything but normal. I am extremely proud of that, and I try to teach my children and my clients that living out of the box, coloring out of the lines and living in the gray is true living.

Look at some of the most successful people in our history, media and pop culture. When they talk about their childhood, when they talk about their life, their success usually stems from a conversation or a story about how they didn't fit in.

I tried repeatedly, and no matter what I did, I

just couldn't. I finally got to an age where I started believing in myself enough to accept and embrace my uniqueness and be confident and comfortable with it. Could you imagine a world where you did? Where you sat back and made a list of everything that made you unique, everything that really made you, you, made the people that love you, love you, and helped you every day in your life?

Also, these could be the characteristics that make the people who love you crazy, but that's okay too. There's something extremely powerful in that. If you want to be as well-known, influential, successful and wealthy as Oprah, those are things to strive for, but do it your way. Do it your way and embrace it your way.

4

SHE LEVELS HER WATERS

"*T*o be at peace within yourself when times go well is easy. The test is finding your calm when life is stressful and overwhelming." —Galit

THE WOMAN with *The Successful Woman's Mindset* recognizes she must have balance in her life to keep herself calm in chaotic times. No matter if you are a mom, entrepreneur, wife, girlfriend, employee, stay-at-home mom, CEO, or any combination of these. How do you feel after a long day of running around and taking care of everyone else and their needs? Do you ever feel like the weight of the world is on your shoulders? Many days I would feel this way: the business, the kids, their activities, homework, cooking, cleaning, creating and meeting everyone else's needs would, at times, take the breath out of me. And the crazy part is I would be worried about all these things and stress myself out before I even walked in the house for the day. I was blessed to observe a father who carried the weight of the world on his shoulders at work and a mother who carried the weight of four kids on hers.

One thing that stuck with me about my father and how hard he worked was the process he used when he arrived home from work every day. The process he used to step away from the pressures and stress of work and almost separate that from himself and what he brought into the house before he was mentally home. My memories go something like this: He would walk quickly into the house, I would barely even see him, and he would make a beeline straight to his bedroom. What I noticed on his way to his room was he was a man that looked like he had the weight of the world on his shoulders. What I saw next was my father walking out of his room, without his briefcase, in his house clothes, with a huge smile on his face. He transitioned from work mode to home mode and became completely present, leaving the weight of the world in the bedroom with his work clothes. It was as if the mere, simple task of taking off his work clothes, putting down his briefcase and putting on house clothes completely shifted any kind of day he had at work.

This, to me, became the meaning of leveling your waters. What does that mean? That means that no matter what happened in your work day, you choose to come home and really be present with your significant other, your children, yourself. I started this ritual myself the moment I started to work and follow it still today.

I also have memories of a mom who worked just as hard raising me and my three younger brothers. She would pick us up from school, cook dinner, do homework with us, take us to after-school activities, attend PTA meetings, volunteer for school and other organizations and somehow, she always seemed to keep it together. It was rare for me to see my mother fall apart or stressed. My mother would level her waters with music, dancing, concerts, date nights with my father and family vacations. You could say I am a combination of both my mom and my dad. I always knew I wanted to have a family. But I also always knew I wanted to be an entrepreneur. At times, this would take a toll on me, trying to be everything to everyone. I wasn't always the calm, patient person I am today. There were days I would walk into the house after a long day at my business office and wonder how I would be the mom, the wife, and all my family needed me to be.

While I juggled work with homelife and raising my three children, I would take breaks by taking a walk, stepping into the backyard, or even driving ten minutes to grab some iced tea. Leveling your waters is about recognizing the need to step away and have a practical break between your current mindset and the mindset you want to transition to next. Leveling the waters is how you live more in the moment, how you stop worrying about what happened, and about what needs to be done next.

My mother would cook, clean, run four kids to and from school and activities and make sure everything on the home front was taken care of. I always remember her being present for anything we ever did or needed. How did she manage that? No matter how much stress she may have been under, she made sure when one of us kids had a question, needed help with homework, or wanted to share something exciting about the day, she would stop what she was doing, take a deep breath, look us in the eyes and respond. I learned to do the same. Even today, my children remember instances where all three of them would be trying to talk to me at the same time, and I would softly say, "STOP, okay, one at a time (and point to one of them), GO." There is something extremely magical when you can level your waters and stay in this exact moment. That is the beginning of *The Successful Woman's Mindset*; recognizing that the past is the past, the future isn't here yet, and the present is where you want your mind and yourself to live. This is where you will prosper the most.

This chapter is about living in the moment, no matter how busy you are or how much you have going on. As I am writing this book, somehow my kids today are 14, 18, and 21. It all seems like a dream. My question for you is: Are you truly living in the moment? When your son gets in the car after you had one of the hardest days ever at work and he is excited to share with you about how his day went at school, are you *really* listening? One of my favorite things to do as a mother has always been to pick up my kids from school because they would get in the car, so excited to share with me the details of their day. I always made sure I was completely present. I reacted, listened, and responded. That is the basis of my relationship with my kids today. My son is finishing his last year of his bachelor's degree and calls me from school multiple times a week just to share exciting news and, at times, ask for advice.

Are you worried about all the things that happened at work (the past) and all the tasks you need to take care of when you get home (the future)? When you walk in the door after a long, tiring day at the office, and your significant other is waiting with a smile to kiss you, is your mindset already in that kitchen or still trying to figure out how that problem at work may be solved?

As a woman who started her own company and had her firstborn by the age of 24, I remember day after day feeling completely behind on everything in my life. Can you relate? Those days you look at the cluttered counter in the kitchen, the sink is filled with dirty dishes, the laundry hasn't been done for days, the children want dinner now, your daughter has a science project due tomorrow she forgot to tell you about and of course, don't forget work or your business and the never-ending list of to-dos.

At the time, I thought I was nuts starting my own business and family so young, and now looking back, I am pretty sure I was right. I was 24, I had a six-week-old baby and took on one of my first commercial properties to manage. My son was sitting in the bouncer next to my computer; I was holding the landline phone in one hand, typing with the other, and bouncing my son in his bouncer with my foot. It was not easy. Can you relate to a day when you were multitasking, and somehow it felt as if you were doing ten things at once? Were you really completing any of those ten things? That day you walked into the house from your job after the worst day at work where nothing went right, and the second you walked into your home your kids and husband could not do anything right either?

The wiser I got (never older) and with experience, I learned to leave work at work. If I worked from home, I would make sure there was almost a ritual of leaving work at my desk. I have developed several little rituals that help with that separation, even symbolically. Being out in nature and spending time outside under blue skies near green trees, getting in the car and taking a quick drive and then coming back home are some of the methods I use to help me leave work at work. What takes you out of your own head? What could you do to disconnect from the hectic outside world in order to walk into your home calm instead of stressed. True, the house scene is crazy too at times! I remember days where my two boys who are less than three years apart would fight so much my daughter would hide in her room to get away from the fighting. Now that my oldest is 21, I can say I am thankful for those days. Especially when the house is pin-drop quiet most of the time, I miss those days. Keep in mind that work, your business or your job are not the memories you will remember when you are sitting in a pin-drop quiet home and your kids are older and have moved out. For that reason, I made it my mission in life to build my business around my children and make sure I cherished every moment with them. Even the moments where my two-year-old would throw herself on the ground and have a meltdown. I vividly remember, on the days I would come home stressed out and overwhelmed, I would bring that energy into the house and it seemed indirectly to be picked up by my entire family. It would change everyone's mood. When I started leveling my waters years ago, everything changed in my household. There was more calm, laughing and bonding.

If you don't have children, imagine for a moment a time where you walked into the house or the office and your mood was stressed. Did it affect the way others started behaving toward you? Did you start bickering with your loved one for the silliest things? It is possible for your stress to impact the people around you and the way you interact with them. Do you remember a time when someone you work with or live with was stressed and then within a short period of time your mood started matching theirs?

Close your eyes for just a moment and imagine this: After a long day of working at home or your office, you find a way to level your waters, to not allow the stress to overwhelm you. You take those deep breaths, take a shower, go for a walk, whatever it is that works for you. You make a **choice**, everything starts with a choice, to embrace the moment and be completely present when you first encounter friends, family, your kids or pets. **Embrace the moment and be present**. Imagine what a positive difference that would make.

5

SHE UNDERSTANDS WHAT MATTERS

"*W*hat Matters is that we should achieve what we set out to do." —Indira Gandhi

A SUCCESSFUL WOMAN'S Mindset is crystal clear on what matters in her life. If you do not know what matters, how can you possibly make it a priority? It could be wanting to grow your company, it could be wanting to stay at home and raise your children. There is no wrong answer. It is your life, and you have a right to live it your way and spend your time on what matters to you. Knowing what matters to you is the first step to choosing to make those things a priority.

Even if it is a plan of action that will take time. Not knowing what matters results in gliding through life with whatever shows up and dealing with it as it comes your way. The problem with this could be that one day you wake up and look back on your life and wonder what happened to the memories, your loved ones, your goals, your dreams.

Do you think your loved ones will remember when you picked up takeout and didn't cook, or when they had to wear the same pair of jeans a second day in a row because the laundry wasn't done? Or when the counter was cluttered, or the carpets weren't vacuumed? As a mother, I have learned those are not the things that even cross my kid's radar. Let me share with you the things that do come straight out of my kids' mouths: My daughter was in the car with me the other day. We were backing out of a parking spot and when we were half-way out of our spot, another car decided to back up and almost hit us. I beeped my horn calmly, he stopped, and we continued on our way to her school, unharmed. What she said next was priceless. Bear in mind she is 14 and a teenager, so her perception is mind-blowing. I said, "I am amazed at how I can stay calm in chaotic situations." and she in return said, "Mom, that reminds me of when we were at the lake and about to get on the boat before it was pulled into the water (she was five then) and the back tire of the trailer was on fire. You calmly said to everyone, we probably should grab some water bottles since the tire is on fire." These are the moments your loved ones remember. The way you spoke to them when you walked into the house after one of the longest days of your life. The way you shooed them away when they were trying to share something special that happened in their day. The way you choose to react when they made a bad choice that day but chose to be honest with you.

The things your significant other remembers are not if you ordered in or cooked, if the counter is clean or dirty. He will remember if you came home stressed out from work and lost your temper with him because he didn't take out the trash before you walked in. Think back to your childhood for an example. More than likely you remember if your parents listened to you or not more than if the house was clean.

What else do they remember? When you took time out of your crazy work schedule to attend their volleyball game. That time you decided last minute, even though you really shouldn't have, to take a day off work and go on that trip to the mountains. Memories are made from the way you speak to your loved ones, the time you choose to spend with them, and the special moments you make together. That is what matters. Your business, job, the house–I promise it will all still be there tomorrow. Experiences, memories, your family, and loved ones. Life comes and goes too quickly. Missed moments matter.

Ask yourself what matters to you? Tomorrow, the next day, next year? What matters to you? Quality time spent with your loved ones, putting away your phone and walking in nature or responding to those ten texts that can wait until tonight or even tomorrow? We live in a fast paced, "must get back to everyone at this exact moment" world. Honestly, I think we get people used to that quick-response habit. When you step back and don't, everything can change.

Think of your calendar appointments and how you follow whatever is in the calendar for the week almost religiously. Imagine for a moment you schedule in your calendar what matters. Imagine if you stopped allowing the things that consume your time to be your life and made sure you set aside time for the things that are important to you. It is an amazing feeling to get to the end of the week and look back and feel like you did what you must, but you also kept the focus on what matters to you.

The Successful Woman's Mindset is comprised of balance. Balance within the things that are important to you. As women, our nature is to compare ourselves to others that seem happy and successful to us. What we don't realize is, you never know the true story of what is happening behind closed doors. Wouldn't it make more sense to stop comparing yourself to others and instead really understand and embrace what being a successful woman means to you? I have seen business women be jealous of moms that get to stay home with their children and not work. I have also seen moms that wish they could go to work and are jealous of business women. Instead of envying others, what if you formed the idea of what matters to you and incorporated that into your life? Work, family, kids, your own business, volunteering or any combination of these or none of these. That is the beauty of your life, it's *yours*.

Balance can be a tricky thing. If you think about it, how many people have balance in their lives? Sometimes it seems as if we finally are getting balance in our work life, but then we don't have balance in our personal life. Or, we're finally getting balance in our personal life, and spending time with our loved ones or ourselves, but now our business is lacking. Or we spend more time spiritually, or in our religion, but then all of a sudden we're not spending as much time creating. None of that is real balance, it's a juggling act.

When you figure out what really matters to you, the path opens for you to incorporate those things into your life in the right measure. Knowing what is important to you is the first step to everything that matters.

Here is a great exercise to figure out what you want: Carve out some quiet time where you will not be distracted and make a list of everything you want in your life, without thinking, with no limitations and no boundaries. It could be what you want right now, or it could be in the future. Write down everything that comes to mind when you ask yourself the question: "What do I want in my life?" If you struggle to find answers, go a step further and split your list into categories before you start, such as business/professional, relationships, health, personal. Once you feel you've explored everything, read through it and pull out three things you want the most *today*. This list will help you identify what matters the most in your life and you can start to focus on your top three things. Keep this list near and add to it as you please and watch how you incorporate things from the list into your life.

6

SHE EMBRACES HER VALUE

"*B*elieve in the value of yourself and your decisions and it's a game changer." —Galit

THE SUCCESSFUL WOMAN knows there is value in everything she does. Why does someone decide to take one job over another? Maybe because it will give them the opportunity to do something they love, or they need the money, or it will help to advance their career. Why does someone decide to start their own business? The personal freedom it can afford, motivated by a passion or wanting to help others. There is value to every decision you make. It is important to know what the value is so you can continue to have the determination and drive to keep at it.

I remember many times in my 25-plus years as an entrepreneur where I absolutely lost my mojo. During those times I had to figure out a way to motivate myself, and it wasn't always easy. I had to remind myself the value that made it worthwhile to me. The values of working in my business were that I could stay home with my kids when they were sick, I did not have to listen to a boss tell me what to do, I got to plan my vacations around my children's school holidays and more! When you evaluate and understand the value you receive from the choices you make in your life, this in turn will push you to have mojo and to find it when it's missing.

Whether we consciously know it or not, value plays a role in every decision we make. You may disagree with me, thinking, "That is not true, I do not do everything in my life because of what I receive in return." I must disagree with you. You may not realize the underlying meaning behind why you are motivated to do something, but it is always there. You may not consciously decide to do something because you calculate what you can get back, but the value and meaning behind it is always there.

I love giving back to my community by volunteering, planning events for women's shelters and much more. When I decide to spend my time giving back, I don't consciously think to myself, "What the value is I am receiving in return?" It is subconscious motivation. I feel good when I do for others. The value or meaning for me is the way I feel doing something good for someone else.

Take a moment to think about the decisions you make in your life. Sometimes in life, there are instances when we become almost robotic, where we thoughtlessly follow paths that may be easier, and we don't sit back and try to understand the benefit or meaning behind them.

When you have an awareness of the value that choices and actions you make bring into your life, be it in terms of the personal, professional, health, or financial, it makes it easier for you to recognize what to say yes or no to.

Value is the word that is misconstrued quite easily. In our society, many times we hear about people who are out there looking for value in everything that they do. I don't want that to be, in any shape or form, what you may think I'm saying here. We've talked about balance. We've talked about what matters. And we also know that at some point, we only have so many hours in the day, especially if you like to get a good night's rest (which is a must for me).

What I see time and again when I work with my clients is that many of them struggle with saying no. Usually when you're a giver, you want to help others as much as you can, but at times it's okay to say no. As a self-professed giver, it took me years of giving and giving to learn that it's also okay to receive. It is important to know not just the value of the decisions you're making, but your own value. The two concepts are tightly connected.

Let's start with the value of the decisions you're making. I get asked quite often, "How can I make a good decision?" The answer: You must ask yourself, first and foremost, what value do you receive from the decision you're about to make? Let's take an example. I get invited on a regular basis to business networking events, but

I choose not to go to every one I'm invited to. If I did, that's all I would do, all day long, as there are enough events to take up all my time. If I did that, I wouldn't have time to spend with my family, in my relationship or on my business.

So, when I receive yet another exciting invitation, I ask myself, "What would the value be to me to attend this specific event?" Sometimes, it's that there is a speaker I am excited to hear. Other times, it's knowing I will get to mingle and connect with certain people I know will be there or people I've met before who have the potential to become future clients. This is the process for my decision-making.

Occasionally, my clients in this stage of learning the Mindset start feeling bad, worrying that turning down an invitation might reflect badly on them. Remember, in business, if the other person is like-minded, the only thing they're going to think is that you happen to have another commitment such as a meeting with a client, or are spending time with your daughter, or any of a thousand other entirely plausible possibilities.

When you're confident in your decision-making abilities, others don't question when you say no. Many people feel as if they must give an explanation and a reason. I don't. I just say, "I'm so sorry. I won't be able to make it," and usually the returning voice is appreciative, "No problem, Galit. I hope you can make the next one. Thank you so much for considering it."

The next step is knowing your own value. Your value is important for you to know, especially if you start your own business or have one. It is common for others to ask you for advice and want to be around you, but if that's your value, why would you continue giving it away? Don't get me wrong, I give away my value a lot because I love helping people, but I also know my boundaries. I give my value away to the local shelters when I mentor women, to the young leadership programs, when I speak at events held by philanthropic organizations. I share my value with causes that have meaning to me. But I don't give it away all the time.

Remember just a few sentences ago where I mentioned about decision-making, and knowing your value of your decision? Many times, I will ask a client to state it in dollars. Why? Because we seem to relate our value to monetary terms. I will ask them, "How much does it cost you to keep that employee that you know you should let go?" And we sit down and put a dollar figure on it. Or, "How much does it cost you to continue to do X?" or, "How much are you giving away in your value every time you allow someone to take you out to coffee for an hour and pick your brain when other clients are paying you for it?"

Every time I have a client complete this exercise, she sits back and realizes she should look at making a different kind of decision, a decision related to the value she has to offer. What you could do at this point is sit back and figure out your value. If you don't know it, look for it. What are others in your field charging per hour? What are others in your profession getting paid?

If you're a stay-at-home mom, what is the value of the education or experience you have if you enter the workforce or what is the value of a nanny, someone you would bring into the house to do what you're already doing for free? Your value is a powerful thing when you figure out what it is.

Spend a few minutes figuring out your value in your business, your job. Choose a category where you may not know your value and focus on it by writing down everything you bring in value. For example: If you are working for someone, write down in detail the service you provide, your unique perspective, what value you bring to that company. This is a great way to start realizing and becoming aware of your value.

7

SHE KNOWS HER WHY

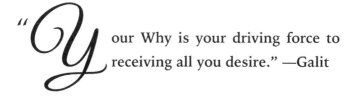

"*Y*our Why is your driving force to receiving all you desire." —Galit

THE SUCCESSFUL WOMAN'S Mindset understands that the *why* is her driving force, her inspiration for passion, creativity and action. I get asked quite often "How do I find my why?" There is a process to it.

Many of my clients do not know their why when we start working together. Having had to motivate myself from the time I was a young 21-year-old entrepreneur, I have learned that the *why* is what motivates you and pushes you to succeed.

What image comes to mind when I say your *why* is your driving force? I immediately think of a speeding car. Total side note: I had a Mustang convertible when I was 18 for about a year and a half. It was the most fun car I ever had. Convertible top down, wind blowing through my hair, driving to the lake with three girlfriends, there wasn't a worry in the world! When I think "driving force" I think back to that Mustang convertible.

When you are clear on your *why,* you are driven to make sure nothing stops you. You jump over hurdle after hurdle. You find solution after solution to whatever obstacle shows up.

The *why* is where you need to start. The *why* will inspire you and it'll also help you inspire others. You are one of my whys. I never imagined I would write a book. I never thought I had anything interesting to share that someone would want to read. And yet, here we are. As a result, you found the title and the topic interesting enough to pick it up. There is something in this book, the back-cover blurb, the title, something that inspired you to learn more about *The Successful Woman's Mindset.* You, dear reader, are my why.

What *why* will inspire you to have passion, to live every day as you choose? To be happy, successful, driven? If you would had asked me when I was younger if I was creative, I would have told you, "You mean stick figures? Oh yeah, I can draw a mean stick figure." In all honesty, I can't even draw a legible stick figure. I am one of the least artistic people you will ever meet when it comes to taking a vision and putting it on paper with crayons, markers, pencils, paint.

But that has not stopped me from trying. I have multiple paintings where I had an instructor guide me. I know I am creative in my writing. I know what my strengths are. I have recognized I'm a writer. I love writing articles and speaking. I have learned where I'm creative.

Your *why* will push you to be creative in the ways necessary for you to do the work you would like or to have the life you choose. Action is essential to incorporate your why. You can talk all day long about what you want to do, the impact you want to have, but if you don't take action, then what? It's just words. All of us know one person who says they're going to do something, and they never do. It's a pet peeve of mine. If you tell me you will call me next week to set up lunch and you don't, don't tell me you are. If you tell me you're shooting for the stars and want to accomplish a goal and you don't, don't tell me you're shooting for the stars.

Action is one of the biggest pieces of my life. I know what I want. I want to inspire, I want to create, I want to make an impact. I put it into practice. Ask yourself what *you* want. Answer yourself. I want to (fill in the blank) because (fill in the blank). Action is the piece that connects all the reasons you have your *why* and all the ways your *why* will push you.

I am sure you have heard this type of question many times in your life: *Why* do you want this job? *Why* do you think we will make a good couple? *Why* do you want to volunteer on this project? You probably hear it more often than you realize. The reason this is a question asked often is because knowing your why will drive you, it will give you determination and be a powerful tool when you have lost your mojo. When you adopt *The Successful Woman's Mindset*, the *why* is one of the most important pieces to your success.

I remember the first time I was asked to speak on stage, as calm as I may have looked on the outside, my insides were ready to crawl out of me. My *why* is what helped me look calm and got me on the stage to make the impact I wanted to make that day. I knew that in order to make that impact, I had to get on the stage and share my expertise and my message. My desire to have an impact was my why that day. Your why will change with every situation or it may stay the same throughout. I am often asked what my why is in general situations and many times my answer is my children. I want them to know they can be whatever they desire in life and do whatever they put their minds to. I want them to know the only thing that may stop them will come from inside themselves; it will not be anything or anyone around them. This is my message on stage as well. In those moments when you are filled with fear and are about to walk away from an opportunity, having clarity of your *why* will push you through.

Do you see a theme yet? To accomplish *The Successful Woman's Mindset*, everything begins and ends with you. You need to be completely self-aware of yourself, what you want, your value and value in what you do, and your *why*. When you are aware of these things, there is a solution for every obstacle you encounter or excuse you come up with to not do something you want to do and to not pursue something you want to accomplish.

How do you figure out what your *why* is? You ask yourself the question out loud or in your mind. "Why am I here today at this meeting?" "Why do I want to give back?" "Why do I want to be the CEO of this company?" "Why am I interviewing for this job?" Many of your answers at times may be logical, but other times you will respond with your heart. If you are allowing yourself to be true to who you are, your inner voice will respond to you. At times you may not want to listen, but when you do, the most extraordinary things begin to happen in your life.

Your *why* will be one of your most powerful tools to reach the *Successful Women's Mindset*. Your *why* will be what gets you out of bed in the morning. Your *why* will be what pushes you when fear and resistance show up. Your *why* will be your self-motivator.

It is important for you to be so clear about your *why* that it almost becomes second nature. Be so clear that it immediately shows up the second you start resisting a new opportunity, a new relationship, or something that is uncomfortable and makes you second-guess yourself.

As a result of my own personal evolution and transformation, I have now become someone who experiences something uncomfortable almost every day. That's okay with me because I know that **growth only happens in the uncomfortable**. It's not a new concept. I'm sure you've heard it repeatedly. The exercises in this book are designed to push you to examine the uncomfortable questions in order to help bring you to *The Successful Woman's Mindset*.

Some of your whys may change and some will stay the same. For example, my children will always be one of my whys. But other whys may change over the years. Ten or twelve years ago, one of my whys was my career in commercial real estate. I love working for myself and finding commercial properties for buyers.

My *why* today for my career is that I want to empower women. I want to impact the world in a positive way. I want to show people they can live their life the way they choose to. When your *why* changes it will likely change to better suit you as you continue to grow. It is important to remember that most people don't know what their *why* is, and even when they do, it can change and evolve as they do. Ultimately, what is important is that you know it is common for you not to know what your *why* is and for it to change at times throughout your life as you grow.

The most common answer I get to "What is your *why*?" is a question in return: "What do you mean what is my *why* My *why* for what?" So a different question that will help you to focus on an answer would be: "What is your *why* for living? What is your *why* for getting up every morning? For motivating yourself? What is your *why* for the decisions you make every day in your life?" The answers to those questions will help guide you to answer the broader question of "What is your why?"

Think about it. What is the reason you're doing what you're doing? Now, for some people it's just about money. For women, it's often more than that. For many women, it's about affecting, mentoring, giving back, proving that you can go to the next level in your business and life.

Many times, a client will say to me, "I want to be successful and I know you can help me and empower me." The first thing out of my mouth is, "Why do you want to be successful?" That is usually followed by complete silence. At that point, I make sure I stay quiet as well, because it is important at that moment for that person to listen and hear the question and reflect. Why do you want to be successful?

The answer is usually along the lines of, "Well, because of this or because of that, or because this person is this way or that person is that way." I repeat, "Why do you want to be successful?" If you ask yourself that question and you don't get an answer right away, it's okay. It's a process. Instead, what you need to do is step back, look at your life and break it down. What are the things in your life that are your *why*? Make a list of your reasons for wanting to succeed, your *why*. Your *why* will be your driving force. Your *why* will be your mojo. On those days when you're unmotivated, you don't want to get out of bed and don't want to do something, that will be what pops into your head, and it will be what pushes you.

Another way to find your *why* is to make a list of all the parts of your life, personal, financial, professional, health, etc., and decide which parts of your life you would like success in. Then you pick one topic and ask yourself *why*. How many stories have you heard of women who are losing weight and changing their lives? Their *why*? "I want to be around longer. I want to see my grandchildren. I want to be able to walk up the stairs and not get tired." There are many whys.

For me, the earliest why I can remember in my life would be the first time I held my first-born. I was twenty-four and the labor lasted for 11 hours. I held my little baby boy in my arms, looked him in the eyes and I knew he was my *why*. I knew one day when he would say to me, "Mom, this is what I want to be," I would say to him, "You can be whatever you want." Today, my son is a college graduate and working for an amazing company as a project engineer. I knew in that moment he would be one of my strongest whys. As a mother of three, I'm extremely blessed to have two more of those. Having two boys and a girl, I want it to be my legacy to show them there is no obstacle or limitation they can't overcome, and there isn't anything that can stop them from their definition of success, except the limitations they set on themselves.

Find your *why*, write it down, embrace it, have pictures of it, and always keep it close. Your *why* may continuously change or stay the same, as long as it drives and motivates you, that's what matters. One of my other whys in the last few years has been watching other women become empowered and overcome their obstacles. By sharing my own obstacles and challenges, my vulnerability and my authenticity, this shows women they can overcome their obstacles. Many times, when I interview a businesswoman or share a live video, and one person says, "Thank you, that resonated with me today," that is part of my *why*. That is what I see as successful. Ask yourself what your *why* is and what is going to let you and allow you to see yourself as successful.

I am often asked why I want to be a public speaker? My answer is not the one that is expected. My path to the stage was in a sense chosen for me. I never said, "I want to be an author or public speaker or anything else I am today." I just knew my *why* was you. I knew I wanted to inspire others to use their voice, to share their story, to pay forward their expertise. What is your *Why*? How do you plan on using your *why* to accomplish *The Successful Woman's Mindset*?

8

SHE IS OPEN TO THE POSSIBILITIES

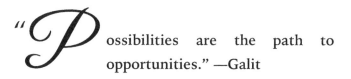

"*P*ossibilities are the path to opportunities." —Galit

THE SUCCESSFUL WOMAN'S *Mindset* is open to the past, present, and future. The successful woman accepts the past, recognizes her present situation, and is open to directing her future.

The key phrase in the second sentence of this chapter is, "Open to directing her future." Many women I speak to don't completely understand that they are in control of what their future can be.

When I write "directing her future," I think of a movie. I love movies. I love watching dramas. I love watching romantic comedies. I love watching inspiring movies. And I always think of the director.

The director can take the script that's written and if he doesn't completely agree with what that writer is trying to accomplish, he can change the content by the way that he directs the movie.

Now think about your life for a second. Why couldn't you be the writer and the director of your own life? Have you ever sat back and just written out today what you would love your life to be like as if it were already true? Isn't that what a script is all about? They write the story as if it were already made into a movie.

Then the director comes in and directs it. We, as the viewers, are watching the movie, we can understand what was in that script. What if you did the same for your life? "Open to the possibilities" is about you; the way you see your life and how you would like it to be, as well as open to the opportunities that show up for you.

What does that mean? Don't expect to stay home and do nothing about wanting more for your life. People will not just show up at your door and start knocking and offering you opportunities. That's not how opportunities work. You must set up the groundwork for them. If you sit back right now and think about directing your future, what kind of movie would your life be? I'm talking about your future. Not about your past. Your future. It can be any story you want.

Why do so many people think their life story has already been written? Shouldn't it have the possibility of being changed based on your definition of what you'd like your life to be? Once you know, you put it into action and then the action opens to the possibilities. It's one of my favorite things to do with my clients. Sit back and put together the story, the description, the visualization of how they can see their future. Or how they would love to be able to see their future. If you can't see it clearly at this moment, that is fine. But it is possible to be clear about what you want; then it happens because that means you're open to the possibilities. Yes, there are a few more steps in between being open and accomplishing it. But honestly, that's the how and I always say, "That's the easy part."

"She is open to the possibilities" is the name of this chapter but will more than likely scare away a few readers because you may not be sure if you are. Are you ready to open your mind to the possibility of learning a different way of thinking? Are you ready to learn the way to have a successful woman's mindset? This question is the most important: Are you ready to explore what is already inside you? My hope is this book will wake up that part of you by giving you the tools to achieve the success you desire.

If, while you are reading this book, you come across something that gives you the feeling of "that doesn't resonate with me," ask yourself if that's a resistance to possibilities and change. This book requires you to shift your mindset, and opening your mind to new concepts can be scary. Try. Be open to the possibility that there might be one idea in each chapter that could have an effect on you which will lead you to a transformational experience.

There have been times that I have gone to listen to a motivational speaker and sat there and chuckled inside, thinking, "I already know that." I had to step away from that and tell myself, "Wait, are you saying you're not open to the possibilities? Are you saying you know every-thing? That there is not one thing you can walk away with from this woman who's getting up on stage, sharing her passion, her purpose to inspire even one person in this audience?" Every time I have that conversation with myself, I am able to hear something inspiring that I could translate into my life. At times it's relevant, at times it is not, but I always learn something.

I believe we can learn something from everyone, but don't misinterpret that to think everything is positive. Sometimes I learn, "Oh, I never want to do that in my life," or, "No, I never want to be that person," or, "I never would speak to someone in that way." That's okay, too, because that's a lesson as well.

As you read this book, ask yourself, "Wait, maybe that is something I can add to my life." Try it. Remember, growth happens in the uncomfortable. Growth happens when you're open to the possibilities. If you are not open to the possibilities, I suggest you examine why you aren't. Then sit down and make a list of all the reasons why you're not and all the reasons why you should be. Then revisit this book. An open mind will give you the best chance to explore *The Successful Woman's Mindset*.

The word "possibilities" can bring to mind many associations. For me, the first word that comes to my mind is "limitless." I love the word "limitless" because it gets me thinking about the idea that we live in a world, especially in the United States, where opportunities are limitless. By extension, many of our limits are put in place by one person, ourselves. The opportunities you have been given or you have worked for are yours, as are the limits that have stood in your way.

Think about it. At this moment, you could probably come up with 1,000 reasons why you are not deserving of or do not have the success you want. Those are self-imposed limits. What if, instead, you chose to look at yourself in the mirror and said, "In this moment, I recognize as long as I allow myself to be open to limitless possibilities, I can succeed." It will be you. You are the one who will stop you from having the opportunities. You will be the one who limits yourself from jumping into action, taking the steps necessary, learning, asking for help, finding the right mentor to show you the path. You are also the one who can bridge the gap between your dreams and your reality.

It is important to understand that being open to the possibilities does not mean you know all the ways how in this moment. It just opens you up to the idea that it's possible. Sometimes just knowing that it's possible, just having the hope and the desire for something, will be one of the most important steps you can take to starting down the path of having the life, the business, the relationship you desire and deserve.

My challenge to you in this chapter is to embrace your potential and possibilities. Recognize that it starts with you, and it starts with believing and being aware. The rest can be figured out.

Many of you may already be successful. That's wonderful. I consider myself successful. I remain open to reading, I remain open to learning. Open your mind to the endless possibilities not just of this book, but anything that could teach you, empower you, inspire you, push you and support you.

Are you ready? Are you open to the possibilities? Answer out loud: **"YES!"**

9

SHE BELIEVES SHE CAN

"*M*y self-esteem is high because I honor who I am."
—Louise Hay

OF ALL THE personality characteristics of *The Successful Woman's Mindset*, believing in yourself seems to be one of the most challenging for most women. I'll talk a lot in this chapter about how we can believe in others, our children, our significant others, our friends, our parents but we always struggle to believe in ourselves. I don't know that there's a secret formula for just magically believing in yourself. Sometimes it's a matter of a "fake it until you make it" attitude.

Why? Because if you push yourself to say out loud, "I believe in me," that sometimes can be the start, even just saying the words. Many women have a hard time saying out loud to themselves, "I believe in me." Try it over and over and over again. Now look in the mirror when you do it. Even more difficult at times.

I don't imagine for a minute that believing in yourself can happen overnight. What I do know is it's my goal and passion that every single woman in the world believes in herself. There's something magical that happens when you start. What is that magical something? A realization of no limitations. No limitations on anything you desire or wish to accomplish in your life or within yourself. You look in the mirror and you accept yourself for who you are in this moment. Instead of looking in the mirror and dissecting all the things that you may not like about yourself, you look in the mirror and you realize, "I believe in me."

When you're about to do that thing that scares you the most in your business or your life and you say out loud to yourself, "I believe in me," that's powerful. Many of us are blessed to have others that believe in us. That in itself is a gift. However, I know from experience that it doesn't matter how many people I have that believe in me. If I don't believe in myself, I won't get up on that stage and share that story. If I don't believe in myself, I won't keep growing my business. If I don't believe in myself, I won't take care of myself the way I deserve. It doesn't matter how much other people believe in you if you don't believe in yourself.

When you start believing in yourself, you don't just believe in the things you want to try to do, you also believe in your worth and in your value. That is when everything starts changing. What happens is those around you feel your confidence. Suddenly, you won't settle for that relationship that's less than you deserve. You won't settle for that job where someone treats you unkindly or unfairly. Believing in yourself is the beginning of everything that you've ever wanted.

There's something about self-talk that is quite powerful. When you wake up in the morning, tell yourself how magnificent you are. Before that big interview, tell yourself you believe in yourself and you are getting the job. Right before that blind date, tell yourself "I believe in me, and

I deserve someone who's wonderful." I learned a lot about self-talk when I went back to graduate school to get my master's degree in therapy. Self-talk can work for you or against you. Those negative thoughts in your mind that tell you, "you are not worthy, you can't do it and you will fail, that is a great way to make sure that nothing positive ever happens for you." Positive self-talk that reinforces a strong belief in yourself is a surefire way to reach heights you never imagined. Make sure that today you start on the journey. That is one of the things I want for you the most.

I cannot emphasize how many women come to me with wishful comments of "I want to...," "I dream of...," "I wish I could, but I don't believe I can..." With that mindset, how do you start believing in yourself? You must have confidence in what you want to do. Confidence can be built. It can be built with tools. It can be built with education. It can be built with resources. It can be built with a support system. You must have the positive outlook that you can believe in yourself. Even if you don't at first, just say to yourself, "I will learn how to believe in myself. I believe in myself." And you must have patience.

The first memory I have of not believing in

myself was during my sophomore year in high school. I decided I wanted to be a cheerleader, and at the end of my sophomore year, I tried out for cheerleading for my junior year.

I went to the daily practices for a couple of weeks. I practiced every day. I showed up, I did my best. We had a few weeks to prepare for tryouts. I practiced front handsprings with a friend. I remember seeing the boy that I liked in the stands watching me at practice and wanting to impress him.

Then the day of tryouts came, and I didn't go. I stayed home, laying out in the backyard and thinking to myself, "I don't believe I can." I regret not showing up. I regret it still today. The good news is that a year later I decided to try out again. This time I resolved to follow through. I tried out, but I didn't make it. The accomplishment was that I pushed myself to believe that I could try out, that I had a chance to succeed. That is my first experience of not believing I can and then shifting my mindset to believe I can.

Do you have a story that is similar? It's common for us women not to believe in ourselves. All day long we will believe in others: we believe in our children, we believe in our spouses or significant others, we believe in our siblings, our parents and our friends. We tell them they can be anything they want. But when it comes to ourselves, we typically aren't our own biggest cheerleader. If anything, our minds work against us many times a day.

When you realize that you have a mindset of not believing in yourself, take a step back and ask yourself why that is. If fear pops up, that's okay, now you know you're scared of what you want to try to do. If you don't think you're good enough, maybe you're comparing yourself to other people. If you're listening to what that person said to you that said, "You're not good enough, you're not going to do it, you'll never be anything," now you see why you don't believe in yourself.

I will tell you from experience with myself and from the experiences of hundreds of women who I've spoken to and worked with, it all needs to start and end with you believing in yourself. If you don't, you will self-sabotage yourself. It is proven every day of the week. You will find a way not to accomplish your goals. You will find a way not to accept that promotion, not to go on that date, not to write that book, not to get on stage and speak. You will find a way because you don't believe in yourself.

How many of us struggle with patience? That has been one of my biggest lessons in this journey because sometimes I want it right now. You must have patience with the process and the journey. Trust in the process. Know that right now it might not happen, but in six months or a year, you are very likely to get there as long as you to choose to start now. That's realistic. It's the things that are worthwhile and meaningful that take time. If you believe you can, you're halfway there.

As women, we are natural caretakers and are quick to support those we love: our friends, significant others, children and so on. If someone needs us to believe in them, we are there. If you are a mom and your child came up to you and said, "Mom, I want to be an astronaut." you will more than likely say, "I believe in you, and you can be or do whatever you put your mind to." Read the last part of that sentence again: "...your mind to it." Isn't that you telling your child to have a successful mindset? Then why can't you do that for yourself? Why can't you believe in you?

Think about how many times in your life you told someone you believe in them. I know I have hundreds, if not thousands, of times. Then think about how many times you said to yourself "I believe in me." If you ask me why women have such a hard time believing in themselves, I would say it's tied to a lack of confidence. There are probably many times where you have had little confidence in yourself. I believe when you try something new or something you've never tried before that is when having confidence in yourself becomes more difficult. How do you become more confident in yourself? How do you believe in yourself? What if you thought of it as just words, "I believe I can," "I believe in me." We don't always see the power of saying certain words out loud and hearing them for ourselves.

Think of the old adage of how to set a child upon the path of success or failure. If, from a young age, a child is told they can do anything and be anything they put their mind to, you are setting them up for success, you are not imposing self-limiting thoughts on them. If a child is continually told they are not good enough and won't amount to anything, this more than likely will affect that child's belief in themselves when he/she is an adult. That's how powerful words can be. That's how powerful your inner voice is. It's never too late to start hearing the right words and voice, and what better way to hear them than within you.

Positivity is not easy for most women. Why? It seems our brains have an easier time venturing to the negative than it does to the positive. Think about the last time you said something positive without a "but" afterward: "This place is beautiful, but," "I love going to the beach, but," "I'm so thankful for... but," "I love you, but." Why is that? Is it possible the reason is directly related to why we can't accept compliments? Are we wired to be happy, to be positive? Or is there a place where we almost fear the possibility of complete positivity because we're just waiting for the other shoe to drop?

As a self-confessed control freak, patience is a quality I have learned to develop as I have gotten wiser (never older). When you want everything, you also want it this second. I want it now. Patience is at times quite challenging but is a must for *The Successful Woman's Mindset*. Patience and hard work go hand in hand toward positive concrete results.

I get asked often by clients or women who hear me speak at an event how they can believe in themselves. My immediate response is you have to go within. Then the next question usually is, what does that mean? You need to look in a mirror and say to yourself, "If this woman, man, company is ready to pay me for my value and hire me, then I am the expert." This needs to be your go-to thought, because recognizing how others positively perceive you will help you begin to believe in yourself. Then you can ask yourself, "Why would I think I am not qualified enough to be an authority on this topic or in this industry?" That is usually linked to fear of failure or even fear of success, which can cause you to self-sabotage. Many of you ladies have gone through major life-changing experiences in your personal or work lives. Our first thought is usually, "I don't believe in myself, am I good enough?" Then fear and self-sabotage show up.

For those of you that are mothers, think of how challenging being pregnant for nine months can be. Labor is not easy. It is not simple to be a zombie for who knows how many months because you don't sleep at night. But you survived, you were strong enough and somewhere inside you, you believed you could.

My mom said to me, "You can be whatever you want to be, Galit." I believed it. I want you to think back to when you were a child. Was there a time in your childhood when a parent, sibling, teacher, friend supported you and told you that you could do and be anything you desire? Not all of us had the perfect upbringing, but I hope there was at least one person you could look back on and know he or she believed in you.

Think back to a time when you dreamt of being something or doing something and you believed, with everything you had, that you could achieve it. If you don't believe in yourself today, go back to that dreaming, go back to when others have told you you're wonderful and brilliant. If you do not have those memories or if you do not have that support today, find it. There are people out there who want to support you and tell you how amazing you are. It's time to find them and surround yourself with them.

Think of a time you were a child and believed in something you wanted to do or be. Then make a list of the reasons why you did believe in yourself. Your answers will probably be because you never thought about a failure in the past and you never thought about the anxiety of something going wrong in the future.

You know those little kids that climbed the trees all the way to the top never looking down or stopping for a minute? It's because they never thought about the challenge of climbing down. It amazes me. I want you to really think about that. Why is it we spend so much time today thinking about all the things that could go wrong when we want to do something new? Taking a risk can be terrifying at times.

Last week I lived for five days in full-blown anxiety and I still did everything I needed to do. I have diagnosed anxiety, but I do not take any medication. Instead, I take natural vitamins, meditate and work on my mind. Most people deal with their mind working against them. I am at a point in my life where my mind is working for me. It's my body that's working against me. My body goes into full-blown anxiety, which nobody usually knows because I have practiced methods for dealing with it.

Many of us don't look in the mirror and talk to ourselves the way we talk to our children, to our significant others, to our closest friends.

Why? Why do we not choose to speak to ourselves the way we speak to others?

The answer is those negative thoughts in our head. Why is it easier to have negative thoughts than positive? Does anybody know? I think the answer is that it is easier to believe the negative because it feeds our insecurities and allows them to remain in existence. The moment we stop feeding them with negative self-talk, our insecurities die. There's almost a self-satisfaction to negative thoughts and then seeing them be validated.

When we come into this world, we are innocent. I'm baby crazy, and the reason I'm baby crazy is because when I look into a child's eyes, there's so much innocence and beauty. There was an adorable little boy sitting next to me on a recent flight. He was three years old, with red hair and big blue eyes. He was the cutest thing in the world, he could not stop asking questions, and he was absorbing everything. Children are like sponges. Why do I love babies? Because they haven't been tarnished by peers, by unsupportive family members.

We live in a world of people who are not all good and no one can get through life without being hurt at some point. That's why it is hard for us to believe in ourselves at times.

There are days when I get in the car (and I swear if you were sitting next to me, you'd think I was nuts) and I say to myself, "You are amazing. You are brilliant. You are beautiful. I love you."

I want you to come up with something that works for you every morning. I don't always have an opportunity to look in the mirror because when I'm looking in the mirror, I'm usually putting on my makeup really fast and straightening my hair, but I want you find a moment to look at yourself and speak to yourself kindly.

Say to yourself, "I am strong. I am beautiful." Whatever it is that you are struggling with, I want you to positively tell yourself what you would tell anyone else that you love.

Another common question I get asked often is "How can I control my negative internal thoughts?" My response is to talk to those internal thoughts, raise your voice at them, yell at them, scream at them. I don't care what it takes. You can retrain your brain. You can work on your thoughts. I am at a place in my life where it's rare that my thoughts work against me. Instead now they support and drive me to succeed.

I cannot tell you how much time I spent in the bathroom last week. I can't be more genuine and authentic than that. My poor stomach, I experienced many new things last week. I spoke for the first time at a new event on a new stage. I traveled and was around people I had never been around. Your body will fight tooth and nail. Your body wants to keep you in a bubble, in a cocoon, and it wants you to be safe, it wants you to be comfortable.

True magic happens in the uncomfortable space when you embrace the butterflies. Imagine saying out loud every single day, "I believe in me." I get chills just saying it now. "I believe in me." It is powerful, and it will work with your internal thoughts, helping you to believe in yourself every day of the week. The more you do it, the more it works on that fight-or-flight instinct that happens in your body. If you want to truly be living your dreams it is important to recognize you must adjust to this feeling.

When my anxiety shows up, I talk to it. I ask it why it is here. I tell it everything is fine and sometimes it's just chemical and I recognize it and let it go.

Then I decide I will not give it any power over me.

Anytime you start giving negative people or thoughts in your life space in your head, you are giving them power. Take back your power. Make a choice. If you don't believe in yourself it's perfectly fine to recognize that others believe in you. It is also important for you to start working on believing in yourself at the same time.

Here are some practical steps on how to get your internal thoughts to work for you: The first step is gratitude. All day long, you need to be thankful for what you have. This morning I struggled with technology for 40 minutes, trying to get online to teach a class in my intensive where 20 women were waiting. When I was finally able to connect, I said, "Thank you." Every night before I go to bed, I say "Thank you," and it doesn't matter what you believe in. I say, "Thank you for my children's health. Thank you for getting us through the day. Thank you for peace and happiness. Thank you for all the things that you give me every day." There are days where I get in that hot shower after a long day and I say, "Thank you for this hot water." I have air-conditioning and a heater. Do you know how many people don't have air conditioning and a heater? I'm thankful I have a car and I'm thankful it started. Gratitude attracts more gratitude, and more things to be grateful for.

Have you ever had a morning where your alarm didn't go off? You get out of bed rushing and you run out of the house upset. The first thing in your mind is "I'm going to be late to work. I'm going to hit traffic. There are horrible drivers out there. I'm absolutely having a horrible day." This leads to everything you thought would happen, happening.

Start being grateful for the little things in your life. It helps you stop focusing on the way things aren't going and instead helps you focus on the way things are. When you're grateful, you can see all the things that are going right in your life, and it fills you with positivity. When you're not grateful, all you see is what's wrong, and that keeps you in a negative mindset. But I want you to be grateful and have gratitude. It makes a huge difference in how you perceive the world and opens your mind to see the positive and the success that already exists.

Next, I want you to ask yourself, "Why are these thoughts working against me instead of for me? Is there a reason?" Sometimes it's a warning or a red flag. Don't you dare ignore that! A few months ago, my house was broken into. I always turn my house alarm on before I leave and what happened was my alarm wouldn't turn on and I was running late. The go-to would've been just leave and don't turn it on, but something inside said, red flag. I walked around, found the window that wasn't closed all the way, locked it and turned on the alarm. And within an hour someone broke into my house, someone kicked down the front door. The second the alarm went off, they shut the door and left. Nothing was taken. I don't want you to ignore the red flags, but I do want you to pay attention and let go of the thoughts that are working against you. The way you can do that is you can ask yourself why. Why is it I don't want to go to this conference today? Is it because something doesn't feel right about it (red flag)? Or is it because I'm fearful?

As a successful woman you must believe you can. You want to have the confidence, positivity, and patience to believe in yourself.

10

SHE USES HER PAST SUCCESSES TO OVERCOME FUTURE OBSTACLES

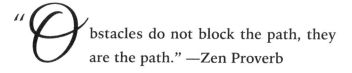

"*O*bstacles do not block the path, they are the path." —Zen Proverb

THE SUCCESSFUL WOMAN'S *Mindset* uses her past successes to overcome future obstacles. There is no force more powerful than a woman determined to rise. When something goes wrong, the successful woman acknowledges it and then gets back up and moves on.

How many times have we succeeded in our past with something, but then a new challenge shows up and we don't remember those past successes? I'm guilty of that, I do that all the time. Then I remind myself, "Wait, you did do something that is out of the ordinary." The other thing that sometimes happens to us as women is that we accomplish something in our past that is a success, and we don't even realize it because it seemed effortless at the time. We are not always strong at recognizing where we succeeded.

I remember a few years ago when one of my girlfriends said that she wanted to put together a team to complete a mud runner obstacle course. I heard the word "mud," I heard the word "runner," I heard the word "obstacle," and I froze. I've never ran a marathon or attempted an obstacle course nor anything involving mud. She started putting the team together and I continued to hesitate. Finally, I said, "Okay, I'll do it." That day happened to be the same day my daughter had a dance competition. I was close to using that dance competition as an excuse, and I almost didn't participate in the mud runner obstacle course.

Instead, something inside me said, "Wait, how many times in your past have you succeeded? You have three children, you have your own business, you're in a field where the average age is 40 and mostly male, you're selling multi-million-dollar buildings." I started focusing only on my successes, and I stepped back, and I said, "Let me look at the dance competition schedule." I looked at the schedule, and there was an opening at the exact same time as the mud runner obstacle.

Even though we had to spend the entire day with my daughter at the competition, and typically it was me that took her, I spoke to her dad, and I said, "Can you come to her competition today? Can you stay with her while I leave?" He said, "Sure." I stayed, I watched her perform, I left, changed into my clothes, and ran the obstacles in the mud with four of my girlfriends. Water, mud, underneath the tarps, climbing up ladders, things I've never done in my life.

When I finished that obstacle course, we took our picture covered in mud, I don't think there was a part of me that wasn't. I realized at that moment, that I had used my past successes to motivate me to overcome my future obstacles, figuratively and literally since it was an obstacle course. There was a place to take a shower, I made sure even though it was out in the open that I washed off as much of the mud as I could, changed into decent clothing and made it back to watch her second performance and the awards. I didn't miss a beat.

At times it is easy for us as women to put others before ourselves, and sometimes I wonder if that is just resistance and fear, ways to self-sabotage. That day I recognized I could be everything I needed to be at that moment, as well as overcome my obstacles, by using my past successes.

"Oh yeah. I made it through that training. I made it through that boot camp. I made it through that 5k in the mud." I'm sorry. What? If you want to understand where you succeeded in your past to overcome future obstacles, share with somebody what you've accomplished. My chin usually drops to the ground when I hear the casual comments, "Oh, I just did this. I just did that." Do you even recognize what a success that is? You look at the past success. What you do is you process it and then you duplicate it.

What do I mean by process? Go back to one of the past successes and write down in detail, step by step, what you've accomplished. This is the logic. How did you do it? Well, I reached out, I researched it, I looked on Google, I found the people that would support me, I went to the right organizations. I received the education. Whatever it is you need to do, you want to make sure you write down all the processes you took to get to that success. Next, you write down the challenge or the obstacle you are facing today. Then take that process and duplicate it.

When you take yourself out of the emotion, everything changes. When we have something coming up, we get emotionally involved, we completely lose ourselves in that emotion. Step back and recognize, "Wait, I got this." I'm telling you that "I got this" is so empowering. If you don't think you've got it, call your best friend. She'll tell you, "You got this."

If you can't believe in yourself in that moment, I am positive you can find somebody who does. If you don't have someone in your life that does, find other women who will.

Use your past successes to overcome future obstacles. I'm always amazed when a woman I am speaking to will be so focused on the big picture of something she's trying to accomplish in her life right now that she doesn't recognize all the times in her past she has succeeded. Many of you, I am sure, have succeeded in something or multiple things in your past. What happens as women is we typically do not give ourselves credit for the things that we have accomplished and overcome. Have you ever told somebody else something you have accomplished in the past, something you've overcome, and they looked at you in awe?

It's happened to me many times, where I accomplished something in the past, or overcame something significant in my life, didn't think twice about it, but then I shared it with some-body else, and they were amazed. Try it. It is a special thing when somebody else looks at you and says, "How did you do that?" And you look at them almost dumbfounded.

I think what happens is we get caught up in this moment and overwhelmed with what it is we're trying to do today. We don't even have the ability, at times, to look at it from the outside in. To look at it through the eyes of someone who has had past successes, that has accomplished things, that has overcome things in their past. It completely changes your perspective when you take yourself out of your situation emotionally and physically and look at it from the outside in.

It doesn't just change your perspective, but it allows you to separate yourself from the emotion. From the emotion associated with complete overwhelm and stress.

At first, when I started speaking publicly on stage, in front of a large audience, I would get overwhelmed with the idea, but I thought to myself, "I'm saying yes. This came my way. It's an opportunity. I will figure it out later." Many times, when I'm about to get on stage, I'm pretty calm. Funnily enough, it's after I get off stage that I start questioning myself. After I speak, I spend a few days questioning, and revisiting, and dissecting almost every word I said, the looks on everybody's faces, and what they said afterward.

What I've learned through this process is to step back and think, "Wait, what typically happens after you speak? Someone reaches out and says you did a great job." Someone comes up to me and says, "Thank you so much. I enjoyed your keynote." I get an email thanking me from the person who put on the event. I watch the video afterward of myself speaking and recognize, "I did do a good job. It made sense."

"Obstacles do not block the path, they are the path." Change that frame of thought. They are not in your way, they are part of the way. I always think about track and field, running over those hurdles. I've made it over one, I've only got three more to go. Always think about how far you've come instead of how far you need to go.

This statement can be powerful when you're using past successes to overcome future obstacles. It is common for a woman to accomplish something and move on to the next goal without acknowledging her own success. Sometimes we get commended. Sometimes somebody points it out. We're not always great at just saying "thank you" when someone compliments us about a great job we did. But if you think about this statement, sometimes we are so focused on the next goal we don't stop for a minute and celebrate our successes. When was the last time you did?

One of the things I focus on with my clients, as well as with myself, is to recognize that even a small success deserves a celebration. Take a minute and go for a walk. Take time to have coffee with your best friend. Take a small trip to the lake that might be 45 minutes away. They don't have to be large gestures. I'm not saying every time you accomplish something to go shopping. Don't get me wrong. If you can, you go right ahead, but that's not always practical.

It is essential to recognize, more than anything, that if you don't celebrate you and your accomplishments, why would anybody else? If you accomplish something and you just slide right through, why would someone else think it's a big deal and celebrate you? Stop. Share your accomplishment with someone who will appreciate it, someone who loves you. Let them be excited for you. Let them congratulate you.

We live in a world where, at times, others consider it bragging if you share your accomplishments. If this is the case, you're surrounding yourself with the wrong people. Make sure you are sharing your accomplishments with people who will be more excited than you are for what you have accomplished.

Sometimes, when we set up a goal, we are so crystal-clear focused on how far we still have to go, we don't take the time to stop and recognize how far we've come. This is a big piece of the Successful Women's Mindset. Take the time to stop, almost like looking back over your shoulder and saying "Wait, look what I accomplished in the last year." I had to do this repeatedly to get through my master's degree program. While completing my degree, there were times I was naive to how much schooling I still had left and the details involved. I was so focused on a paper or project that was due next, I did not always pay attention to what lay ahead. I think this helped me not get overwhelmed and focus on the immediate instead of what I still had to complete.

When you're only focused on how far you have to go, it becomes overwhelming. Many times, I will speak to a potential client and just the thought of the steps she will need to take to get to where she wants to go will overwhelm her and threaten to stop her from taking even the first step. When a client wants to meet to discuss hiring me, nine out of ten times within ten minutes of our call she has shortness of breath. Why? Because she is about to embark on something that is not comfortable, and fear sets in. My response is, "This means you are ready, take that first step and break through that fear and the rest is right in front of you for the taking."

Try this process. See what a difference it makes in your accomplishments. Stay in the moment of what you need to finish right now. Remind yourself of how far you have come. Once you're ready for the next step, focus on that. The key here is not to allow yourself to get overwhelmed. To recognize that in the past, when you were succeeding in different areas of your life, you may not have been focused on how far you still had to go. Look back at that success you completed, take this opportunity to recognize you did succeed. There is a process to how you succeeded, but many times, we're so focused on the steps, we don't recognize the accomplishment.

Make sure you take time to focus on what you have accomplished in your life. If it's something you can't see clearly, write it down. Make a list. Make a list of every single accomplishment, small or big. If you had surgery, and now you're walking, focus on those first few steps. If you decided to take the opportunity and apply for that promotion but didn't get it, you still applied for the promotion. That's success. If you were single and you decided to put yourself out there in trying to meet someone, but it didn't work out, you still put yourself out there and tried to meet someone. They don't have to be huge gestures. They don't have to be large steps. Sometimes, just taking the first step is a success, and I want you to recognize that and commend yourself for the small steps as well as the big ones.

11

SHE GIVES BACK

"*I*t's not how much we give but how much love we put into giving." — Mother Theresa

AS A SUCCESSFUL WOMAN, you recognize that part of your success is giving back. What does this mean? It means there are many charitable organizations looking for someone like you to help the people that walk through their doors every day. Someone that has had experiences with difficulty, and obstacles and has found a way to succeed even after these experiences.

Serving others, you recognize as a successful woman that it does not matter what level in your life, you're at, more than likely there's always going to be another woman, or child, or organization that can benefit from your skills and experiences and from your journey. It's interesting, because sometimes when I work with women and show them how to give back to their community, many times they will say, "What do I have to give back?" Or, "I'm not far enough in my career. I am not stable enough in my life. I don't have enough to offer."

What that woman doesn't recognize is, the journey that she's been on, whatever it might be, already has given her the expertise and experience to have the ability to impact somebody else in this world. Many times, when I talk about serving, the response I receive is, "Well, where could I fit it in my life?" Or, "Where do I begin?" Those questions are easy to answer. More than anything, what I want you to know is this: if you have a passion in your heart for something, and most of us do, because most of us are natural care takers and givers, that is where you start.

The moment that you have a passion for something, anything, that's the moment that an idea is born to serve others. The real test is the follow through. If you've been on a weight loss journey, if you've been in an unstable relationship, if you worked hard to leave the corporate world and figured out how, if you have a love for children and want to make sure no child suffers, no matter what their upbringing is, there are many causes out there that are waiting for you to help. Choosing a cause is the easy part once you tap into what you love and what you're passionate about. Once you get started many times what happens is you wish you had more time to give because there will be another cause that is near and dear to your heart.

Make sure not to overwhelm yourself. Make sure to recognize you have the time to give, but it's not something you must choose to do every day all the time. Why? Not because you wouldn't want to, but because you still need to recognize that you want to take care of your loved ones and yourself. There isn't a minimum amount of time I encourage my clients to give back. It's about what you can do, and it could be the smallest gesture or idea that you implement, and could still make the greatest difference, because remember, impacting others can be as simple as impacting one person. That is serving others.

I remember volunteering in the Girl Scouts

from the age of eight to thirteen. Yes, a lot of it was about having fun, learning new things and making new friends, but in addition to that, they instilled in us the importance of giving our time to make a difference. I remember one of my first volunteering experiences at the age of eight, we decided we were going to make care packages for the homeless. We filled a gallon size Ziploc bag with granola bars, cheese and crackers, a water bottle, some toiletries, and each of us Girl Scouts wrote a note of kindness for each homeless person that received the care package.

As a child, I'm not even sure I really knew or understood the impact that volunteering and serving others could have on others as well as myself. From there, it pretty much has been a string of volunteering, board positions, events that I've planned, fundraising I've been involved in. I'm sharing all this, so I can show you another important part of the Successful Woman's Mindset. The Successful Woman's Mindset recognizes that while we can focus on ourselves all day long, sometimes we will get more satisfaction and more joy out of focusing on someone else's needs. Also, she recognizes it isn't always about us and our success. It is at times about others and their needs and about making the world a better place.

Some of my favorite organizations to volunteer for are organizations that support women. Women's shelters that help women with addiction, abuse, mothers with children who are homeless or in a dangerous situation. As an adult, one of my strongest memories of volunteering at a local women's shelter was when I went to drop off donations, I saw a mother with a 1 year old in a stroller. She was asking if they had a jacket for her child. At that time, they were out of jackets (which does happen at the shelter sometimes). She then took a blanket that they gave her and wrapped her child three times so that child would not be cold.

That memory stuck with me. It still sticks with me. It's interesting because I do have a personality that tries to find a need and fulfill it. From that experience stemmed a program in which every year a local donor donates enough money to buy every child in the shelter a new jacket. I could share story after story that's similar. Another program is the back-to-school event that provides every child at the shelter with a new outfit for the first day of school and a new backpack full of all school supplies. I love being a part of that. Is there something you see in the news, or an organization in need that you love to support? That's where you start. You start there, and you ask, "Is there a need I may be able to fulfill that I am passionate about?"

The other thing a successful woman is aware of is that giving, volunteering, and serving is contagious. When you start sharing that you have an event or a program, or collecting items for a charity, it's awe-inspiring how many people will step up because they see you're doing good and you're only asking something small of them. It becomes almost a domino effect that you impact someone that gives, and they impact someone that wants to give, and so on.

Some people think giving back takes a lot of effort and energy. They don't realize there is no secret formula for giving back. Giving back can be from the smallest thing, such as donating toiletries to a local shelter to something grand, such as planning events that raise millions of dollars, and anywhere in between. I have sat on many philanthropic boards, I've helped plan and been a part of planning fundraising events. As many times as I have been told I am amazing for doing so much for others. I think sometimes I'm a bit selfish. Why you ask? Because it makes me feel good to do something and make a difference in someone else's life.

Where do you start? As I mentioned earlier, first start with something near and dear to your heart. For me, its women and children. Then, you start searching your community for organizations, reach out, and find out how you can be on their volunteer list. Sometimes there's a process, but it's not difficult. Find out what their needs are and where you can fill a gap and make a difference. What I can promise you is as much as this is part of the formula of the successful woman and having the Successful Woman's Mindset, you will benefit so much from giving back you will want to do it more, and you will want to do it over and over again.

More than anything, I want you to recognize this chapter is about the idea that your mindset is positively affected every time you see the impact you can have on one person's life. Focus on making an impact on one person's life at a time. This one person will grow into two, and it will grow and grow into many more.

SHE IS A LEADER

"*A* leader leads by example with grace and dignity." —Galit

THE SUCCESSFUL WOMAN recognizes that being a leader is an essential quality to having the success she desires. She is a leader in her own life and through the impact she makes on others in her profession and community.

When I started thinking about writing this book, it came to me so clearly. The importance of leadership is apparent in women that I've met, and features in my own experiences. I am the leader of my life, and I often encourage my clients to choose to be the leader in their lives. I am asked quite often what qualities a leader possesses and should have.

A leader leads by example. If you speak up at a meeting at work, lead from a positive place and share ideas for your team to implement and work together on, you are now leading by example. You are showing others it's not about you. If anything, you're taking the attention off you, you're sharing with them the ideas you have so that you all can succeed.

Another quality of a leader is being a team player. To accomplish your vision, you must have a quality team. I have many visions of things I would love to succeed at, not just in my business but in the philanthropic organizations to which I contribute my time.

One of my goals has been to fill the needs of those philanthropic organizations, but with everything I have on my plate I could not possibly make the impact I would like alone. I realized I need to build a team of amazing people that would share the same vision I have. Recognizing that a team with skilled and talented people to support your work serves to lift you and your team up toward success is being a team player

Hand in hand with the leadership quality of a team player is your team members' strengths. Have you ever experienced a colleague, boss or someone in your life pointing out your weaknesses instead of your strengths? When was the last time someone said to you, "You are amazing at (fill in the blank.)" When was the last time you said to somebody else, "You are talented at (fill in the blank)?" It seems that somehow our mindset is set to point out and notice weaknesses. Well, the quality of a true leader is someone who plays to the strengths of their team members and of those they love. Focusing on people's strengths makes for a more positive relationship and general experience.

Another important quality of a leader is having a clear vision. Once you have a clear vision of where you want to go, it is much easier to put together a team that will help you make your vision a reality. Clarity is the key to sharing your passion for a goal you would like to accomplish with your team. A passionate leader will always have others that want to jump on board for a cause or project.

Many of you may be leaders just like Oprah. You may be out there making a difference, someone who is influencing the lives of those they love and the lives of strangers. Even if high-profile leadership positions do not resonate with you, more than likely there's someone in your life, your job, family or friend that you impact positively as a leader. We don't always recognize how much we lead others because at times we do without a second thought.

Another superb characteristic of a leader is passion. I get told quite often I'm extremely passionate about what I do. If you've ever heard me speak, I only speak about topics I'm passionate about. I am passionate about the title of this book and its subject matter. I can only operate from passion. A true leader operates from passion. I am positive you are passionate about something in your life. Often I get asked, "What if I don't know what I'm passionate about?" Typically, the woman I speak to knows what she is passionate about, she just needs the guidance to recognize it, believe in it and how to accomplish it.

The last quality I want to share with you about a leader is courage. Leaders are coura-geous. Leaders make decisions that aren't always easy. They speak up when others won't. They recognize they can't live in a box to make the impact they want to make. Leaders are not always concerned about pleasing everyone, they recognize that they do their best to please everyone but that it is not possible. They are more concerned with the majority of the team and what would work for them as a whole.

With these leadership qualities, you too can embody *The Successful Woman's Mindset* in recognizing that a true leader will know when to step up or step back, depending on the situation, and when it is time to lead. Leading is not always about being in the forefront; at times a leader must learn to lead through others and the examples that have been set for them. As a leader, you want to make sure you are preparing the next generation of leaders in your profession, and your life.

13

SHE TURNS FEAR INTO DETERMINATION

"*N*othing in life is to be feared, it is only to be understood. Now is the time to understand more, so that we may fear less." —Marie Curie

THE SUCCESSFUL WOMAN is aware of her thoughts, her body, emotions, and reactions when fear shows up. She is conscious of the effect fear has and recognizes it is part of the process of growth and change. She recognizes that fear does not completely disappear with each experience, rather she understands that it is her relationship with fear that changes. She turns fear into determination.

Fear of success, fear of failure, fear of rejection, fear of the unknown. I could mention 100 more fears, and any one of them may resonate with you. At times it becomes a leap of faith to be able to move past fear, and at times it will push you to leap, leaving you no other choice. The other side of fear, the place where it turns into determination, can be the most beautiful realization that the impossible can be possible.

When I work with a client and fear is what is holding her back, I ask, "What is the cost associated with letting fear make choices for you?" When I say cost, I don't mean, cost as in money. I mean cost as in your life. What will it cost you to stay stuck? Will it cost you that dream job or the relationship you've always wanted? Will it cost you a lifetime of missed opportunities? The next time fear threatens to make the choice for you, ask yourself ,"What will it cost me in missed opportunities?"

I have seen fear take away some of the most beautiful things from people around me. It takes away the ability to impact others positively, the potential to grow, the opportunity to be themselves, their gift of using their voice, and more. Honestly, I've been there. I've allowed fear to stop me in the past. My experiences are what have shaped this book and me through learning to turn fear into determination.

I remember many times I wanted to try something new and I was fearful of it. Now, I look back, and there are times I regret not taking a leap of faith. Today, I'm living a different life. I've decided I won't allow fear to stop me. At times, that can be terrifying. But now I'm in a place where fear pushes me. Now it makes me determined to accomplish whatever it is I am fearful of.

This chapter isn't about doing all those adrenaline junkie things that scare you. I have no interest in doing that. I have no interest in skydiving, not because I'm fearful of it. It just doesn't interest me, but there's nothing wrong if you want to skydive. This is about those opportunities that come your way that are unknown and, at times, terrifying. This is about those times you let opportunities you want pass you by, because fear is making the choice for you.

What are the opportunities or risks you would take right now if fear weren't choosing for you? Write them down, then write what the cost will be to your life if you do not push past the fear and turn it into determination.

When someone says, "Oh, I'm fearful of..," I ask them where they feel fear physically in their body. Fear can show up in many forms: heart beating out of your chest, sweaty palms, shaking knees. It can also just be in your thoughts in the form of the "what ifs." "What if I fail? What if I look stupid? What if I am not good enough?"

The next time you feel fear, or it shows up in a situation associated with day-to-day life, pay attention. Pay attention to what happens to your body. Pay attention to what thoughts you have. Then stop, be aware of it and ask yourself, "Does fear deserve to have that much control, does it make sense for it to have such an impact on my life and the things I want to accomplish?"

Do you know that feeling you get when you are fearful of something? You're thinking, "I can't do this, I must say no, I don't have enough experience. What if I fail? What if I don't do well?" This feeling can be turned into determination by recognizing that the power and the strength of it can be repurposed. Take that power and instead of letting it stop you, let it push you past it. Decide that you will come out on top.

When fear shows up, the fight or flight instinct kicks in, urging you to run as quickly as possible away from the thing that you fear. This is an instinct in our body to protect us from danger. It is understandable that when something feels scary or uncomfortable, our body wants us to run. If there is a fire, this instinct is important, and you want to listen to it. But what you may not realize is that it also comes into effect with anything new you want to try or anything that might feel uncomfortable. When you are aware of the difference between a life-threatening situation and your fear of the unknown, you now can choose to conquer it. How? Allow the feeling, recognize it and start finding your way toward that one thing you want to try right now.

This is when everything changes because now you tell your body, "I recognize you are fearful because this feels new and uncomfortable, but I am telling you that I am safe."

When fear shows up for me, I get this feeling in the pit of my stomach. Where does fear show up for you? I recognize how powerful that fear is because it's showing up and it's not going away. What I do next is I allow it to feed into determination. It pushes me. You want to give yourself the chance to feel it. I do not believe in sweeping it under the carpet and not dealing with it. You want to deal with it, you want to recognize it, and then you want it to drive you. One of the most rewarding things for me as a woman is getting to the other side of fear. I can tell you from personal experience that the shortness of breath, perspiring, and rapid heartbeat are worth it because right on the other side of fear is everything that you want.

My 14-year-old daughter is so much fun. Yes, she's 14. Yes, I know what you're thinking, "The teenage years." She says to me, "Watch out. Mom's determined." That is a well-known statement in my house. When I get determined, everyone stays out of my way. It's fun to watch my daughter now as she's growing and trying new things, now she gets determined too. I ask if she needs help and she responds many times with, "No, mom. I'm determined." So I step back and let her figure it out on her own.

First, become aware of the fear, then allow the feeling, recognize it, and start finding your way toward that one thing you want to try now. Resolve not to let it stop you. When I came up with this concept of turning fear into determination, quite often I was asked by women, "How can I turn fear into determination?" My answer to them was, "If you think about it, what's the difference?"

Think about a time in your life you were so determined to do something that you weren't going to let anything, or anyone stop you. Most often, this has something to do with someone we love before it has to do with ourselves. I want you to think about that time for a minute when no obstacle, no person, no situation was getting in your way. Think about that place in the pit of your stomach that gets all worked up when you start feeling determined.

Now stop and think about what it feels like when you feel fear, when you're about to do something new in your life, and fear is what's stopping you. Does that feeling come from the pit of your stomach? If you stop for a moment and think about it, our stomach is only so big. Is it possible that those two feelings may come from the same place?

It took me a little while to make a connection between fear and determination. I spend quite a bit of time making sure fear does not stop me from having the things that I want in my life. I get told quite often that I must not feel fear. Well, of course, I feel fear. I'm human. I think the difference is I'm completely aware of my fear so that when it shows up, I have already decided I am not going to give it any power.

To work through your fear and turn it into determination, you first must be aware that it's showing up. How? "I am aware that I am feeling fear right now." Say it to yourself out loud, "I am aware that I am feeling fear right now, and I recognize it." Recognize it, then go a little deeper: "What is it I fear right now? Is it logical?"

I want to share with you the five steps to overcoming fear that I myself use. Some of the most common fears that I have seen in my clients and in those that I have worked with are fear of failure, fear of success, fear of rejection, and fear of the uncomfortable.

The first step is to surrender to the feeling. You don't want to ignore it. You don't want to run away from it. If you're feeling fear at this moment regarding a goal that you want to accomplish or something that you want to do in your life, it will keep showing up for you. Instead of running away from it, choose to sit with it. What does it mean to surrender to the feeling of fear? You become so aware that you recognize at this moment you are feeling fear. Sit with it. Recognize it, allow it, and surrender to it. Sometimes I'll tell my clients to say it out loud, "I am fearful of ... This is what I fear the most." Acknowledgment is a big step in the right direction of overcoming your fear.

The second step is to focus on the goal. At times the big picture can be overwhelming. What if instead you broke it down into the specific details and focus on one step at a time. You start by writing down your goal, then write down the specific steps it would take to accomplish that goal in as much detail as possible. If you are not sure of a step, just do your best. This in itself should take away some of the overwhelm. Also, remember to write down the end goal at the bottom of the page and how you will feel when you accomplish it.

The third step is to let go of the what-ifs. Be in the now and recognize that the what-ifs are what's stopping you. We are so focused on the next thing that can potentially happen, the what-if, that we don't give ourselves an opportunity to stand still for a second and recognize the idea or goal can actually happen. How do you let go of the what-ifs? You make a choice to stop thinking about them. I want you to know right now that you have the potential to be the best in the world at coming up with the what-ifs. We are experts at coming up with the what-ifs that we let it overpower what we're trying to accomplish.

The fourth step is to focus on the end result you are trying to accomplish. That is your reward. On the other side of fear, you can accomplish the desires you want most and find the opportunities that you dream of. Sometimes I tell my clients, "Work backward." Imagine yourself there. Imagine what it will feel like to accomplish your goal. Let's say it's a 5k race. Imagine what it will feel like at the finish line, not how long it will take you to train, how long it might take you to run and all the what-ifs in between. The reward of feeling and seeing yourself at that finish line, when you focus on that end result, helps push you. It turns that fear into determination.

The fifth step is to take action. The fifth and final way through the fear is taking action. Once you're on the other side, focus on how you did it and what it felt like afterward. That will reinforce the reward of pushing through the fear. This prepares you for the next goal. There is no secret to not ever feeling fear. Instead, focus on recognizing fear can be helpful, fear can be turned into determination and that each time you get past it, you have more chances at getting closer to the next goal you want to accomplish. It prepares you to get past the fear quicker and not let fear dictate your choices.

Many times, when fear is what is stopping you, there is no logic behind your fearful thoughts. Make sure to listen when the thoughts are logical (your red flag). But when fear shows up and it stops us from something that we know in our gut we want to do, that's when it's time to turn it into determination.

The best way to test this theory is to pick one small thing you want to try that's new. Then try it. Pay attention and notice the feelings you get in your stomach and the thoughts you have when you're trying. Because fear will show up and try to stop you. Then you want to make sure you work through it. Pay attention to it, notice it, recognize it, and work through it.

There is no force more powerful than a

woman determined to rise. I believe that when you get determined, others will get out of your way. How many times has your husband or significant other said, "Oh, I'm going to get out of the way of this one?" At the end of the day, that's what happens when you find your determination.

14

SHE GIVES AND IS OPEN TO
RECEIVE

"*I*t is a gift to give to another, it is another's gift to you when you choose to receive." —Galit

THE SUCCESSFUL WOMAN knows how to give as well as how to be open to receiving. Wait. A lot of you might be thinking, "I'm open to receive." But are you? Are you wholeheartedly open to receive? What does that mean? Support. Mentoring. Guidance. Someone to believe in you until you can. Recognize you don't have to give back each time you receive. Recognize you have something to offer. If somebody wants to give to you and wants to help you from a loving perspective, you accept it.

I put into practice everything I share with you. I have some of these concepts down and some of them I'm constantly working on. The receiving part has been a big one for me to master. People come out of the woodwork saying, "Hey, do you want to speak?" "Do you want to put on a workshop?" "I would love to connect you with…" I say okay and then I figure it out afterward. That's accepting.

As women, we're not always good at saying thank you. It took me years to respond to, "You look beautiful" with thank you. "You are brilliant." Thank you. "You are amazing." Thank you. Don't downgrade yourself. Don't take yourself to a place where you say, "Oh, well, I could've done it better. There could've been more people. I should be more successful." Thank you. It is a beautiful thing. That's you receiving. If you ever think twice about starting to go into that negative spiral, think about how you're taking away that compliment from the person who gave it to you if you don't just respond with, "Thank you."

They made an effort to compliment you. By

denying their compliment, you are undermining their perception of you, their kind gesture and yourself entirely. "Thank you," allows them to give and you to receive.

"She gives as well as she is open to receive." What does this actually mean? I'm not talking about tangible gifts. We want to offer our time, our knowledge, our expertise to others. It doesn't matter to whom, be they family members, business associates, or philanthropic organizations. When you are open to receive, you recognize that to be a successful woman and to have the mindset, you may need to ask for some help and thus, so is the case for others.

It always surprises me when I get a call from a woman whom I consider to be ahead of me in business who says, "I would love to learn more about what you do." My initial thought is usually "Oh, they're probably trying to sell me something." But no, they just wanted to connect me with different people in different fields they thought would benefit me.

There are times when I receive and I keep thinking, "Well, why? Why do they want to do that?" If you're the kind of person who loves to give to others, why do you? I know why I do. I love giving to others because it satisfies my desire to help, support and mentor. Don't make the mistake of only giving away your value and never charging for your expertise. You must know where your boundaries are. But at the end of the day, women empowering women, women supporting women, means we have to be open to receiving so others can give to us in the manner we give to them. This may be in terms of advice or networking connections. You don't know what it translates into until you open yourself up to receiving.

In my career, I have always loved reaching out to women that I admired. I've also had younger women reach out to me wanting to learn how to be successful in their career or business. My goal is to reach as many women as I can, to give them guidance and direction. On occasion, a young woman would reach out to me in my commercial real estate business and ask, "How can I be a commercial agent?," I made sure I took the time to either connect by phone or meet in person. It wasn't unusual to later see that same woman or hear about her succeeding in the profession. What a great feeling that was, it was a win-win each time.

I have been hired as a mentor by many women who needed the tools and the guidance to succeed in their business or profession.

By the same token, I have hired women who are where I would like to be. That is remaining open to receiving. I want you to ask yourself if you are open to receiving from others. If you are not, you are missing out on a world that is beautiful, supportive and will believe in you. There are organizational groups to get involved in and other women who would passionately mentor you. Why would you close yourself off to the potential? You never know what is on the other side of receiving. I have had the most wonderful things come into my life because I am open to it. Make sure that you are too.

How can we be open to receiving? Many times, we think that asking for help or reaching out to someone who may know something we do not know is a sign of weakness. In all honesty, if you think about it, isn't that a sign of strength? Admitting you may not know enough at this moment shows the strength of character to acknowledge that your knowledge is lacking and to search out the expertise you desire. As a past self-professed perfectionist, I must share with you that I struggled for years to allow myself to receive. I'm a natural caretaker and giver. I'm a mom of three, and I've always taken care of my children and the man in my life. I am the oldest of four siblings, I have three younger brothers. I have a blend of the entrepreneurial spirit as well as a little bit of Betty Crocker in me.

For me, it was a struggle to understand that I needed to be open to receive. Have you ever felt like somebody was closed off to you or someone didn't like you? That's an energy that you feel. People feel your energy. If you're presenting yourself as someone who knows everything and isn't open to receiving guidance, information or connections, then others will not reach out to you or offer you opportunities.

I have opened myself up to the possibilities of receiving from others in my life. Not just in my personal life but also in my business. There isn't a week that goes by where someone does not reach out to me and say they want to connect. I am open to receiving that connection. When you are open to receive, you now have the ability to take a moment and decide which connections will benefit not just you, but also the person reaching out. Not all connections will be a fit.

Part of *The Successful Woman's Mindset* is knowing which ones to follow through with. You are aware there are only so many hours in the day and you must choose how you spend them wisely.

I love giving. What a great experience to be open to receiving connections. It results in potential speaking gigs, clients that are referred to me, opportunities to present. There's something remarkable that happens when you make a point of being open to receiving. It is an important quality of *The Successful Woman's Mindset*.

There are times where I will be working with one of my business clients and I will say to them from the outside it looks like their client list is full and they'll say to me, oh no, I have room for more clients. Make sure it's known. Make sure you're putting out there that you're open to receiving potential new clients. Then I'll see that client post on social media sites a video that says, "I have room for three new clients in September, let me know if you're interested in x, y, and z."

That is making it known you are open to receive. You don't always need to publicly state it, but sometimes, why not? If you don't put it out there, how are people going to know?

15

SHE OWNS HER MISTAKES AND FAILURES

"*T*o Fail is to take one step closer to success." —Galit

THE SUCCESSFUL WOMAN recognizes owning her mistakes and failures is part of the journey. She recognizes there's no way to know what success is without failing. When you fail, you have something to learn from and compare to, then you know what works and what doesn't. We've all heard it, we've all seen it: famous people in history who have failed. Walt Disney, the man that gave us Disney World and Mickey Mouse. Did you know his first animation company went bankrupt? Did you know he was turned down 302 times before he secured financing for creating Disney World? If he had stopped at 301, we never would have had Disney World, Disney movies, and Disneyland.

Another great example: J. K. Rowling, the woman who brought us Harry Potter. Did you know she was rejected 12 times before *Harry Potter and the Philosopher's Stone* was accepted? Twelve times. What if she had given up at 11 and decided, "I'm done." She would never have the empire she has today, and we never would have had Harry Potter.

I, myself, have failed many times in my life. What I've chosen to do is recognize that it's part of the journey, and I accept it. I don't dwell on it too long. I know I'm not successful in everything I do, so why not instead adopt *The Successful Woman's Mindset,* which is, "Okay, I failed. So, what? What's next? What can I do differently, what can I learn from it, who can help me and guide me, so I succeed the next time?"

Many of my workshops are successful and full, but initially, I marketed some of my first group programs for months and not one person registered. Not one. There were some workshops I had to cancel because only one person registered. Each time I did not succeed, I looked at what I needed to change. I saw accepting my failures and my mistakes as an opportunity to learn and to grow. Imagine seeing them instead as an opportunity to grow in place of a disappointment. Everything changes when you shift your mindset. Now when I fail, as they say, it's back to the drawing board to try again.

If you need motivation? Google people who have failed and are successful today. Actors are a great example. Think of how many auditions most actors have to complete to receive an acting opportunity and they keep at it, rejection after rejection. Authors, too! They are rejected dozens of times or more before a large publishing house agrees to publish their work.

What needs to drive you and motivate you is learning from those mistakes and failures and accepting them for what they are. Yes, there are things you will not have control over, and there are times you will make a mistake or fail. I choose to look at myself and see what I can do better moving forward.

I can't even tell you how many TEDx Talks said no to my proposals. I hadn't had that many no's in my entire life because I've always worked for myself, and I always knew what to do next, but one TEDx Talk after another said no. I choose to look at every no as a step closer to a yes.

The Successful Woman's Mindset recognizes that we are in a place where some of what's happening in our lives is related to some of the choices we've made. It's important to recognize that blaming others does not solve the problem. Blaming others does not uplift you. You must own your past choices and learn from them in order to move forward successfully.

With the many failures in my life, I have learned to get up much quicker, and learn the lesson intended. I was speaking to some ladies right before a keynote on this topic and I said, "Ladies, it's not about thinking you're never going to fail. It's not about deciding that you need to stop being this type of person or having these types of characteristics. It's about recognizing, 'Oh, wait, that didn't work,' and learning the lesson, learning to get up quicker, and how to implement the changes to be more successful the next time you try."

We are human, and we can't eliminate mistakes and failures. What we can do, is learn from them so next time it's a shorter process to get to the next step.

This is one of my favorite elements-- that the mindset of a successful woman always owns her mistakes and failures. At this point, you may be shaking your head and thinking, "What do you mean my mistakes and failures? Why do I need to own them?"

There's something powerful about a woman who recognizes she makes mistakes, but it's not just about recognizing it. It's about voicing it and taking responsibility and not dwelling on it. I have made many mistakes in my life, in my career, relationships, as a mother. I am human. As I get wiser (because you know it's never older), I recognize it's not about the mistake or failure. It's about how I choose to handle it, and what I learn from it to hopefully avoid the same thing happening again.

In my business career, there were many times I didn't handle a situation in a way that I could be proud of. I look back and I learn from it. I can say (if it's to myself or the colleague I interacted with) "I am sorry I did not handle this in the best way," or "I recognize this mistake is on me."

As a commercial real estate broker, the real

estate division holds the broker responsible for any errors or mistakes that a real estate agent makes working under their license. At times, this does not feel fair. How can I control what my agent does? I can't supervise them 24 hours a day, seven days a week. But think about that statement and why that law is in place. It is my job to train them. It is my job to supervise them. It is my responsibility to know what kind of person is working with me.

If I am not aware, then how can they be good at what they do? If I don't give them the right training or direction, how can I blame them when they make a mistake? Of course, there are always exceptions to this. I've had times in my business where employees I trusted were fraudulent and misused credit cards and checks.

Even in those situations where there was no way I could completely control it, I now can look back and know what checks and balances should have been in place so maybe I could have avoided the fraud or the behavior. As I said, you can't always avoid it, and there's no way I could've known.

What is important is owning your mistakes and your failures that are in your realm of control. You make choices and sometimes, based on those choices, the outcome may not always be positive.

What you want to do is step back. You want to step away from the emotion, and you want to recognize what choice you may have made that lead up to the mistake. Many times, you can't do anything about the mistake because it's already come and gone, but what you can do is step back and learn from it. That is the biggest take away I want you to get from this chapter.

For me, at this point in my career, I have arrived at a place where I expect myself to make mistakes and fail. Please don't confuse this with the idea that I set myself up for failure. Oh no, I don't. I set myself up for success, but at times failure will occur. It is about how quickly I choose to learn from it, so next time I know better. I think of my mistakes as lessons and my failures as opportunities to grow.

Think about how powerful that is. You don't give yourself a hard time, you don't beat yourself up, and you most definitely don't get stuck repeating that failure or mistake over and over again. Rather, you recognize it, you transform it into a lesson that you learned so you can take that lesson forward with you to your next big mistake. That might sound funny, but if you really think about it, the most successful people in the world have failed and failed again. To make mistakes is to be human.

I know that to be successful I must fail. How can you know what works if you don't? How can you succeed if you don't? Mistakes are part of the path, they're part of the process. Choose to learn from them. Choose to grow from them. Choose to accept them.

16

SHE GETS COMFORTABLE WITH THE UNKNOWN

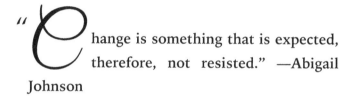

"*Change is something that is expected, therefore, not resisted.*" —Abigail Johnson

THE SUCCESSFUL WOMAN welcomes and embraces the unknown. She trusts her intuition and gets out of her head. Recognizing that the unknown future should feel exciting, not uncomfortable. I am a creature of habit. I love eating at the same restaurants, visiting the same places, and doing many things that are comfortable for me in my everyday life. That is just who I am, and there is nothing wrong with that if that is who you are too.

This chapter is about not allowing the uncomfortable feeling you may get from new opportunities to stop you. Part of the exhilaration of the journey is when your heart beats out of your chest and you just can't breathe. To me, that is living.

I most recently took my 14-year-old daughter to New York City for the Broadway experience. I had never traveled that far alone with her on a trip to an unfamiliar city, just us in a hotel together, exploring the unknown. The uncomfortable feeling was in full force and working overtime for me on that trip. I entered cars with strangers (a car service I hired through the hotel) and went to places I had never been. If you'd been with me, you would have never known. I was calm, making smart decisions, but the unknown was ever present. The difference is, I did not let it stop me from planning the trip and did not let it stop us from having one of our most memorable vacations. When was the last time you did something exciting and unfamiliar that made your heart beat in excitement?

Do you like the unknown? I wouldn't be surprised if almost 100 percent of those reading would answer NO. At the end of the day, most of us like to know what will happen. We like to know what is coming.

The mindset of the successful woman is open to the unknown, which allows anything to show up. For good or for bad. Be prepared and know you can handle whatever comes your way, no matter the obstacles or hurdles. Don't approach it with "That's not positive. This is going to be bad. What if, what if?" Instead, simply be prepared and aware. Bad can happen, but good can too.

There's something beautiful about a woman who is in front of an audience or a business meeting and something goes wrong, yet she knows how to stay calm, how to work her way through it. It's just a part of life and it's a part of the natural course of living. I do not have a tool that I can teach which will avoid every mistake or failure in your life. But I do have tools that will help you navigate through it calmly and as best as possible if and when it does happen.

Most of us are not comfortable with the unknown and can only approach it with baby steps. That's okay! For example, I went away to San Francisco a few months ago. I used to be the kind of woman who had to have every moment of every trip perfectly scheduled. This time, all I had planned was the hotel and the flight. Nothing else was planned for the entire time we were in San Francisco. It took me baby steps to get to that space.

I become more comfortable each time I do this. Now, I don't plan what I do when I go on trips. I just go. When we arrived in San Francisco, I approached the concierge and said, "Hi, we'd like to book a time to go to Alcatraz during our stay." The concierge looked at me like I was nuts. "Oh, people book that months in advance." I said, "Well, Sunday at 2:30 works." I flashed him a huge smile.

He looked, and to his surprise he responded, "Okay, no problem. There happen to be two tickets, someone must have canceled." Everything worked out on that trip. It was better than I ever could have planned it. This is what I mean when I say test the waters. Do something slightly different with a small amount of discomfort, and then move on to a bigger action step. There's something extraordinary about embracing the unknown.

A comfort zone is a comfortable place, but nothing ever grows there. One of the first things

I always tell my clients is, "You're going to get really uncomfortable while working with me. Get used to it, because if you want to grow as much as you say you want to grow, the uncomfortable will be your new normal." If you want to grow, the unknown and uncomfortable should be your new best friends.

One of the things that keep women stuck in their life and their business is the avoidance of the idea of exploring the uncomfortable. Being in the comfortable and familiar can lead you to be stagnate and remain stuck. Through my years as an entrepreneur, I have learned to be more and more comfortable with the uncomfortable. That might sound a little odd, but if you think about it, what a great perspective to have. What if you choose to become comfortable with the uncomfortable? What if instead of allowing yourself to feel stuck in your life or business, you embrace it, you recognize it, and you're open to it?

The most incredible things will happen in your life when you do. Time and time again in my business, something would show up that I didn't expect. For example: once I lost five business accounts during the beginning of the recession. Ordinarily, the fear of the unknown would take over, along with the fear of my business income drastically changing. What could I do? Well, I could freeze and worry and let things get worse, or I could face the uncomfortable and get out there and find new clients. My team and I worked together to find new business that was out of the box. Change and growth happen only if you embrace it.

How can you become more comfortable with the unknown? First, recognize that it won't feel good at first. You will want to run the other direction. Running is our coping and defensive mechanism, literally and figuratively. It's what we want to do the first moment uncomfortable shows up. Think about that first date. Think about the first day of school. Think about the first day of a new job. Your heart is beating out of your chest, your palms are sweaty, you can't think straight and all you want to do is run as far away from the uncomfortable as you can.

Next, think about what happens when you work your way through feeling uncomfortable. That's where the magic happens. I learned a long time ago that if I wanted to be someone who grew for the rest of my life, I must recognize not everything is always comfortable. By embracing and allowing uncomfortable to show up in your life, you have the potential and the ability to accomplish amazing things. That first time on the stage or on a trip by yourself for a weekend or any other first in your life can start off uncomfortable and end up as one of the best experiences of your life.

I can name one time after another where I felt so uncomfortable it was as if I was going to throw up. I wanted to hide under the desk. Can you think of a time in your life where you were uncomfortable, but you still chose to say yes? You chose to embrace how you felt? Now think about the other side of uncomfortable where the magic happens, where you succeeded and embraced it and accomplished that goal. It happens when you make a choice to allow uncomfortable into your life, (and when I say uncomfortable, I don't mean that red flag). I mean that place where you know for a fact that the one thing stopping you is fear and you rise above it.

You look that fear, that uncomfortable specter in the eye and you say, "I've got this." "I know I can do this." Then victory is right there for you. Then what do you do? You duplicate the process over and over again because it's so powerful that you want it more and more. For me, becoming uncomfortable has become a normal part of my life in my business because I'm aware of the rewarding results of growth and success. Even more rewarding is how I get to do what I love and at the same time teach people how they can do the same. At this point, I would be doing you and myself a disservice if I didn't choose to embrace the uncomfortable.

This is my first book. Do you know how uncomfortable it is for me to write this? To share with you some of the deepest and most difficult things I have overcome? But if I didn't choose to embrace it, I would never publish this book. I would never have the opportunity to inspire even one person like you to choose to face the uncomfortable to have *The Successful Woman's Mindset*.

17

SHE IS VISIBLE

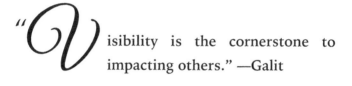 isibility is the cornerstone to impacting others." —Galit

THE SUCCESSFUL WOMAN IS VISIBLE. She recognizes the only way she can make an impact is by sharing her experiences, successes and failures, with others. This could be in business, volunteering, or even leading in her profession or community or any area of her life she wants to grow or impact others with.

A good example would be someone in the spotlight who utilizes their visibility to make a positive impact in the world. For example, Oprah. Her success and visibility has given her the opportunity to bring awareness to many causes, and to donate millions to philanthropic organizations all over the world.

This chapter is about the idea of visibility with relation to a few things. First, if you want to give back and serve you can use your visibility to attract others to do the same. This gives you the opportunity to make an even bigger impact because now you are sharing your vision with a larger audience and hopefully mobilizing people toward your cause. Secondly, your impact through visibility could be from the simplest thing, such as people being inspired to engage with you to effectively help them succeed in their business and anywhere in between. It is essential to recognize that you're doing others a disservice if you keep your talents and expertise to yourself. I believe each of us was given a gift, so we could pay it forward and teach others.

Visibility gives you the opportunity to do just that. If you have a gift that you're hiding and not sharing with others, how can you make an impact? How can you show others how to impact their world and their life in a positive way?

Visibility for many of my clients is something they struggle with at first because they think,

"Wait, I don't want to be a 'celebrity.'" "I don't want to be in the public eye. I don't want to be out there and be vulnerable." Well, that's understandable. At that moment I have them step back and I ask, "Do you want to make an impact? What kind of impact do you want to make? Do you want to inspire others? Do you want to share what you know so others can rise above their own challenges?" Many of the times I ask these questions, the answer is yes, over and over again.

When you let go of the vulnerability of being visible and recognize it isn't about you, it's about the opportunity and capability to make an impact by sharing what you know, this can change your perspective.

Often I will walk the fine line between being visible and hidden. I love that one of my offices is a home office. I love that there are days where I have pin-drop quiet and I can just work from home, behind closed doors by myself. That is the balance I crave because my journey has required me to be visible since I know that's the only way that I can make a positive impact. Which is to impact others, such as you, and share my experiences as I am in this book; this can only happen by allowing myself to be visible.

Know that visibility at times may not feel comfortable, and that's okay. That is another part of the uncomfortable-but-normal part of the journey. Make sure to revisit often the reason why it is important for you to be visible. Revisit what your purpose is, what your passion is and what your journey has been thus far. What a shame it would be if you didn't share that experience with others, so that maybe their journey will be inspired or a little bit easier.

Impact is a beautiful thing. I couldn't imagine a world where those who have the wisdom, the education and the experience didn't choose to share it with those who don't. In our community, we have many groups that support women who are working through suicide, rape, sex trafficking, homelessness, domestic violence, drug addiction and more. Those groups are fueled by women who have gone through the journey themselves and have chosen to volunteer their time to show these ladies there is a way out, that there is a light at the end of the tunnel. By sharing, they show them that there is a way for them to accomplish healing, have the support and guidance they need to have the life that they deserve. That is another way of utilizing visibility, even on a one-to-one basis or in small groups, to have an impact.

Believe it or not, this probably is one of the most challenging Successful Woman's Mindset characteristics for me. I'm someone who's tried to hide in the shadows most of her life. I was the girl who always wanted to push my girlfriends into the limelight. I had friends who were cheerleaders, friends who were actresses and models. I preferred staying behind the scenes and in the shadows. Not because I was fearful of the limelight, but because I loved watching other people shine and I loved supporting them.

What I learned throughout the years was that in order to be a truly successful woman and to model the mindset, I needed to be visible. I couldn't make the impact I believe I was meant to make in empowering other women by sharing my experience and expertise unless I was visible.

This meant putting myself out there, being vulnerable and, at many times, quite uncomfortable. This meant getting up and speaking in front of large crowds, television appearances, writing for magazines. I'm not sure what it means for you. What I can tell you is this: more than likely you have a gift to share. All of us do. That gift is not worth anything if you don't pay it forward. I recognized my gifts, and I knew it was selfish for me to not share them with others because those gifts are meaningful to me only if they impact somebody else in a positive way.

I often say at my speaking engagements, if I impact one person in the crowd and they make a positive choice that day, I feel accomplished. I feel that putting myself out there was worth it.

How do you become more visible? First and foremost, social media makes it easy today. You share about the places you volunteer. You invite and leave open the doors for others to get involved. You lead, recognizing that, many times, as a leader you will be directly or indirectly influencing future leaders. You make sure you are out there with the goal of impacting others positively.

At times, visibility can almost feel as if you're speaking in front of a crowd naked. There are times after I'm visible that I question myself and I question what I said. Most of the time I'm being ridiculous, but I'm human. For some of you, visibility may mean standing up and speaking when others will not about a subject that is controversial. That can be terrifying. But how can you have *The Successful Woman's Mindset* if you don't share your gift through visibility? You may already recognize that this journey isn't always about you, sometimes it is about the impact you make on others, the lives you're going to change.

Remember, *The Successful Woman's Mindset* has many characteristics, and some of these will speak to you and some of them will not. My experience has taught me that to ensure that my message reaches a wide audience, to succeed in having an impact, I had to allow myself to be visible.

When you ask yourself if you should be visible, ask yourself, "Do I want to benefit others?" If the answer is "Yes," then it's time to get comfortable with visibility. There is no right or wrong. I am sharing with you my experiences and what I have learned over the last 20 plus years of developing *The Successful Woman's Mindset*. Visibility is one aspect that has come to the forefront just in the last few years for me, but it is a must of *The Successful Woman's Mindset*.

SHE IS ALWAYS OPEN TO LEARN

"*E*ducation is education. We should learn everything and then choose which path to follow." —Malala Yousafzai

A SUCCESSFUL WOMAN is always open to learning. In today's society, we have the world at our fingertips. Google has made me the smartest woman on the planet. Okay, maybe all of us women are smarter because of Google. When I ask Google, it immediately tells me how to get somewhere, where to buy something I'm missing, the recipe for a dish I want to cook. In today's world, it is possible to find a resource to learn anything we want. If you really think about it, you could spend from the day you were born until the day you die learning something new every day. And many of us do. I know I strive to.

We are blessed to have the opportunities as women in this day and age to learn as much as we want, when we want and about whatever we want. Think about other countries where women are limited in their education. There are countries where women are limited because of cultures and beliefs that control and repress what they are allowed to learn. There are countries where women are limited because they don't have the resources to bring the world to their fingertips and don't have access to the Internet. Then why wouldn't we, as women who are fortunate enough to have freedom and access to education, want to expand our learning every single day?

I'm not suggesting you go out and learn about things that don't interest you. What if, instead, you made a list of all the things you've always wanted to learn? Photography? Nutrition? Medicine? Gardening? Sports? Or anything else that interests you?

This chapter is about the successful woman always being open to learning. Learn about what you want to learn. Learn from those who are around you on a daily basis. Learn from those who are offering to teach you and from those you can seek out to learn from.

We covered in one of the first chapters what the definition of the successful woman is to you. We also covered learning about that successful woman. Why wouldn't you want to learn what it is you need in order to have *The Successful Woman's Mindset*? Learn from this book, from society, from your peers and from those who are out there wanting to teach you.

There are different avenues to learning. It doesn't always mean you need to go back to school. It could be picking up a book, watching a video, attending a workshop, or reading an article. It could even be just listening to somebody talk. When you open your mind and are always open to learning, it just becomes a natural part of every day. You will be open to learning when people aren't even directly trying to teach you.

I have sat down with an 80-year-old woman and learned from her and her history. I've sat down with a 25-year-old woman and learned from what she sees in the world and what she hopes for. Anyone at any age has something to teach us if we are open to learn. It's incredible what happens when you open yourself to learning and recognize you have the ability to absorb information, especially when it interests you.

Let's compare two educational subjects such as math and English. Imagine you love one and not the other. Let's assume you love math and don't love English. Math is easy for you and you love learning it. You walk into the class completely engaged. You want to learn how to solve the next problem. You absorb the lessons every day. English? Not so much. It doesn't interest you. Everything you are taught you just can't grasp. Class seems to go on for hours. Every time you have to write a paper you cringe.

It's important to know what you want to learn and why. Have a list, an ongoing list, and every day try to incorporate something into your life that teaches you. It's unbelievable when you do, the possibilities are endless, and your limitations disappear. The how will never be your problem. You will always find a way to find the how.

I always want to learn. I want to learn for the rest of my life, and the successful woman wants to learn for the rest of her life too. That is the way you continue to be successful and grow in your life. If you're happy with where you are, embrace it and celebrate it. If something inside you is telling you, "I want more," and there's something missing, there's a reason. Typically, what we do is we stay in our comfort zone because we don't want to experience the unknown.

You want to be open to learning. I love learning from other women and seeking them out. There are many amazing women out there. I believe we live in a special time, or maybe I'm just blessed to know the type of women who want to uplift and support one another.

I make a point of scheduling at least two coffee meetings a week to give, to receive, and to learn, or to teach. What the exchange is just depends on the person I meet with and what happens to come up. I'm learning from the women who are learning from me. There's always something to learn. The mind is like a parachute: if it isn't open, it doesn't work. I greatly believe that.

Years ago, I remember I had a client say she was a professional student. I asked, "What does that mean?" She said to me, "I have a bachelor's and a master's, and I've got a minor in this, and a major in that and now I'm shooting for my doctorate."

I said to her, "That is wonderful. Why do you keep returning to school? Why do you keep learning?" she said, "Because I want to learn for the rest of my life. What a privilege to have the opportunity to be a woman and to have the ability to learn. There's so much in the world that I don't know."

That conversation opened my eyes. I recognize that throughout my career, I've always wanted to learn. When you are open to learning you embody *The Successful Woman's Mindset*.

When you open yourself up to the possibility of learning, almost every person you encounter becomes a learning experience.

Some of the things you learn from others you may choose to never use or share. A successful woman recognizes she doesn't know everything, and at the same time, that she has areas of expertise she may choose to share with others that they don't know about. She is aware there's always something more to learn.

I love reading. I love listening to audio books.

I love watching speeches. I love school because I am a sponge for learning. How do you love to learn most?

I'm aware of the areas of interest I have: I want to learn more about being a better person, about personal growth, about how I can work with my clients in an effective way and to teach them all the things that I learn. In order to be open to learning, it means that you recognize its okay to ask, "How can I do that?"

Take a few minutes and make a list of all the things you've always wanted to learn. If you have your own business, what are the areas that are not your strengths? Those are the areas you're going to want to learn more about. When you look at the list of the things you've always wanted to learn, make it part of your mission to educate yourself.

Maybe you love photography and you've always wanted to know how to take great photos. Maybe you've always wanted to be a writer, but you never really knew how to form your words. Maybe you want to be a public speaker, but you don't know where to start. There are many things to learn in this world. One of the concerns I hear most from my business clients is they don't know the "how" to accomplish what they want.

Well, that takes learning. There are enough people out there who know how to do the thing you don't, but in order to be able to learn from them, to be able to search them out, you must be open to the idea of learning. Make a choice. Make a choice to be open to learning always, and then the possibilities and your potential for growth will be endless.

SHE NEVER FEARS COMPETITION, SHE LEARNS FROM IT

"The only person you should ever compare yourself to is the person you strive to be." —Galit

THE SUCCESSFUL WOMAN knows competition will always exist, she is aware there will always be someone with her expertise. The successful woman seeks out those who are more successful in the areas she wants to develop. She never views competition as a threat. She recognizes we are more in competition with ourselves. She embraces we are no different than Oprah or the billionaire, the only difference is what we allow ourselves to comprehend with our own self-awareness.

It's an amazing thing when you accept competition, and instead of fearing it, you let it drive you. When I first started my passion business, empowering women in business, I did not know anything about the executive business coaching world. Then it seemed everywhere I looked online, at networking events and just about anywhere I went all I met were other business coaches. It is in our nature to compare ourselves to others, that is not always a bad thing. What if instead of stopping yourself because of the competition, you chose to learn from it? Why do you think I'm so successful in my business? The reason is because I teach my clients what I have learned as an entrepreneur for more than twenty years. Part of that experience was what competition taught me. It's part of what drives me. Often the competition will support you and collaborate with you or drive you to up your game. Competition shows you that each person is unique in their abilities, expertise, and way of sharing and paying it forward.

If you have ever experienced the cut-throat world of competition, I want to share with you that the opposite world also exists. How do I know? I have lived it in my professional career. When I first entered the commercial real estate industry, I found that some of my competitors wanted to embrace my talents, share with me their experience and support me in my ventures. Please do not mistake this for naively thinking that the cut-throats did not exist, of course they did. They do in every industry, as well as in your day-to-day personal life. It's your job to find the part of it that isn't cut-throat. There is a sister-hood out there of women who want to support you, uplift you and help you succeed.

When I entered this world of serving and following my passion, I allowed myself to be open to the amazing women who were more successful and more experienced than I was. This includes the professional speaking world as well as the business mentoring world. Every single day, I support women and I get supported by women. If you are open to what you need, you will receive it.

How do you learn from the competition

instead of fear it? Competition is deeply inter-twined with fear. First, do you understand what it is you fear from the competition? Do you worry they are better than you, that you are not good enough, that you won't succeed because of them? Once you embrace what your fear is, it's time to work your way through it.

Fear of failure in the face of competition is a common fear. Have you ever felt fear of failure in starting any new endeavor? Have you felt you could not measure up to those already in the same industry or social circles? The first thing you want to do is be aware of it and surrender to it. Many times, as women, we think it's a weak-ness to feel fear and try to push it away and ignore it. Guess what? It will keep showing up if you don't deal with. At this point, just decide to recognize it and say out loud, "I fear failure." Even just typing it is uncomfortable. It is powerful when you acknowledge your fears and embrace them. That is the first step in not letting fear stop you. Instead, turn it to your advantage. Once you recognize the fear for what it is, you can better zero in on the goal you want to achieve. Once you surrender and recognize the fear, you want to zero in on the goal or task you fear at that exact moment.

When I started writing this book, the first 40 pages came so easily and quickly and then it felt like the biggest task I had ever taken on. I tapped into why I resisted and what it was about this book that I feared. It was the competition, the writers who were more experienced than I was. I have never been that great with big words. I was the girl who didn't do so great on vocabulary tests, and my writing (even though I loved writing in school) was always simple. I was concerned my wording would not be fancy enough or expressive enough to interest anyone to read this book. I also feared the competition; it seems everywhere I looked another person had just written a book. How did they get it done so fast? How is it a best-seller? How are they already on their third book and I am still writing my first? Trust me, I wanted to quit multiple times, just about every week. But I knew I needed to stop fearing the competition and instead recognize the opposite. If everyone is writing a book, why can't I? What makes me so different that they can and I can't? They aren't my competition, they are my motivation. Can you see that? Can you see how if you change your perspective from competition to motivation, what a difference it can make in every aspect of your life? It's phenomenal what mindset can do for you. Its mind-blowing how just changing your perspective can change your whole world.

When I was given the assignment by one of my first mentors to research the competition in business mentoring, I did the research and said she was nuts to think I could be successful. I knew I had the experience, I knew I had the ability to mentor, I knew I was a remarkable entrepreneur and business coach. I learned that what I feared the most was starting in my 40s to build a new global business online, when I had worked for so long to build a thriving and profitable career in an entirely different industry. Once I realized my fear of the competition, the rest fell into place. How? I stopped fearing the competition and decided instead to learn about them, connect with them, support them and even at times to promote them. You might ask, why would I promote my competition? The simple answer is because it is strategic to maximize your network of giving and expertise by having others to refer new contacts to if they are not a good fit for you.

I am often called "the connection queen." I connect people to what they need, and my competition connects people to me. Embracing the fear of competition is recognizing that there is a world out there that will not necessarily compete with you directly. Instead, it can teach you, push you and motivate you. That helps with the fear of competition.

I am quite aware of the entrepreneurs out there who are making tens of millions in their businesses, and that has always driven me. It has driven me to recognize if they are doing it, I can do it too.

Do your research, become familiar with your competition, learn what it is that you love about them and what you don't. Then you make it your own. You can only reinvent the wheel so many times, but what a beautiful thing when the wheel can be unique to you and your personality.

The next step would be to visualize the end result of the goal you are aiming for. It's no secret I am a visionary, I see for my clients what they can't. The moment a woman shares with me her dream, I immediately can see her accomplishing it. I don't just see her accomplishing it, I also can logically share with her the steps to get her there. I do not share them at first or all at once because first she must see her vision, see herself where she wants to be. If you were dreaming of starting a marketing firm to help nonprofits raise money for their organizations, fearing the competition or having a fear of failure of the unknown will stop you at just sharing the idea.

I have an exercise I share at my workshops and with my clients. You will need a quiet place, no distractions, and some paper. Close your eyes and envision yourself at a place where you know you have accomplished a goal, something you dream of becoming your reality. Think big, don't hold back. No logic, no boundaries, just the possibility that it can be. Use your senses while you are there: What are you wearing? What do you smell? Who do you see? Can you feel anything? One of the following two things usually happens when I hold this exercise at my workshops. Either the woman will open her eyes and start writing down every single detail of what she saw, or she will open her eyes and start crying because she couldn't see anything. Both reactions are normal and expected.

If you can see the details, you are on your way to knowing it's possible. Make sure to take that vision and continue to see it in greater detail, incorporating it with the action steps to get you there.

If you don't see anything, it's a good idea to revisit what fear is standing in your way. Then go back over the steps to help you overcome the fear. Do not give up on your vision, it's there in your mind, it's just hidden behind the fear and obstacles you have subconsciously placed in your way.

The last step is to take action. You can think about what you want for the rest of your life but if you do not choose to take that first step on your list, even the smallest step, you will never get to your desired action and end result. Sometimes a woman who is interested in working with me will say she is just too busy to do whatever it is she needs to do to make her dreams a reality. There is this underlying assumption that you must have lots of time available to accomplish what you want. What if instead, you found five minutes a day, two hours a week, one full day a week. Whatever it might look like for you. Doesn't that mean you are that much closer to accomplishing what you want? But if you don't start at all, do you recognize you will never actually get there in your reality, rather only in your dreams?

SHE DOES WHAT SHE LOVES

"*B*ut you have to do what you dream of doing even while you're afraid." —Arianna Huffington

THE SUCCESSFUL WOMAN recognizes she spends more than a third of her life in her business or at her job. She recognizes and is aware that spending that much time in a profession and not loving what she does can have a negative impact on almost every aspect of her life.

You've heard the stories and you've heard the comments. "I hate what I do." "It's my 9:00-5:00." "I can't wait for Friday." And so on.

Loving what you do isn't always the easiest

thing and knowing what you love to do is a process at times. I have a presentation called "The Seven Ways to Love What You Do." I end the presentation by saying, "if you don't do what you love, love what you do." I discuss the impact that not doing what you love has on your health, your relationships, and your general mood. None of this is probably a surprise to you, because if you're spending that much time doing something you don't enjoy, of course it will have a negative impact on areas of your life.

The good news is, it is possible to figure out what you love to do and it's also possible to love what you do until you do what you love. No, I'm not trying to write in riddles. What I'm trying to express is this: *The Successful Woman's Mindset* recognizes that to be successful you must be as happy as you can be in each area of your life, and your profession is a big part of that. So, if you're not happy there, how can it translate to the other areas of your life?

Many people say, "Well, I ended up doing this job, or going into this profession because life happened." I understand that. I started my first career quite young. It was an easy and natural path for me, having family that was involved in construction and real estate. I followed the path. But I can tell you I also wholeheartedly loved what I did.

Don't confuse this with loving every second of every day and every single task associated with your profession or business. No, that's not how it works. There are many things I do not like to do in doing what I love, that's not what this chapter's about. For those areas you don't love doing what you love, usually you can find ways of delegating or managing them. I don't believe you can do what you love every second of every day, just as in life, there are positives and negatives to everything. This is about having a career or a business you are passionate about. That most of the time, you just don't feel like it's work. At times, you almost feel bad because you're making money while really enjoying what you're doing, but you recognize your value. Of course, you're compensated for your hard work, even if you love it so much it doesn't feel like work.

How do you figure out what your passion and your purpose are? One of the exercises you can use to find your passion is make a list, no limitations, no boundaries, of everything you love to do. Don't think, just write. Just write everything you love to do that you feel passion for. Then, for your purpose, make a list of what gives you purpose. What makes you feel on top of the world. What is it that you would do every single day that would make you feel like you had a purpose, if money was no object and if responsibilities were not there?

When you have these two lists, you spend time on them and don't doublethink the answers, just write. You cross-reference the lists, you circle what works hand in hand. And now it's time to do your research.

Many times, I'll speak to a woman about potentially working together and she'll say, "I don't know what I love to do." A lot of times you do know. Most of the time, it's the thing you do every single day or talk about the most or already do for free. We just don't realize it can also be something we can get paid for. How wonderful would it be to get paid for doing something that you love? It is an absolute blessing when it happens. When your days turn into nights and you must give yourself boundaries to stop working.

How do you figure out what you love to do? What is the thing you enjoy doing more than anything else in your world? Is it listening to others? Is it gardening? Is it organizing? Is it implementing systems? I could go on and on, but I am sure there is something you love to do more than anything else in your life that can connect with a potential career path or business.

A great place to start, when you're starting to figure out what you love to do, is purpose. Are you interested in doing something that has purpose? Recognize many of us women have this natural caretaker personality and many of us love helping others, love inspiring others, want to uplift others to succeed. That could be in different ways. Not everybody wants to work for the Red Cross or be a therapist or a doctor, that doesn't always have to be the path when you're finding your purpose. For some people, it could be, "My purpose is I want to show other women that it's possible to overcome obstacles that they may have encountered as a child." Or it could be, "I want to make sure that every person in this world recognizes how important health is." For someone else, it might be, "I want to change the industry of the stock exchange and open it up for more women."

If you are interested in operating from

purpose then you first want to figure out what you believe your purpose is. And then the second thing would be passion: "Okay, wait. What am I passionate about?" And more than likely you already know. If you want to work from passion and purpose, it is all possible. It's just really narrowing down what that is for you.

Once you figure out those two elements, it is a great start on the path of doing what you love. Until then, start by changing your mindset. Wake up in the morning and feel blessed and grateful for having a job to go to, for having the income to take care of the people you love and to do the things you enjoy. Then make a plan. I work with my clients on a plan. It could be six months, one year, two years or even more. But you must have a plan if your goal is to work for yourself or change professions or job.

The reality of the world is most of us can't just quit our job and start a new business or go work somewhere else without a plan. But it is possible to have a plan, so you can start to work toward your dream and still have the security of a livable income if that is what you strive to do.

SHE IS A WORK IN PROGRESS

"*T*o be a work in progress is to be a woman open to improving herself everyday." —Galit

THE SUCCESSFUL WOMAN'S *Mindset* recognizes she is a work in progress. She understands and knows that *The Successful Woman's Mindset* characteristics are an ongoing mode of living that can be learned and implemented for the rest of her life. I use this statement quite often in my life, especially in the last ten years. Someone will ask me a question about myself and I'll answer, "I'm a work in progress."

You may notice that the chapter titles are

characteristics of the mindset that will come up at different times in your life and in different situations. But you should also understand that the successful woman is working on her mindset every day in the routines that she chooses to implement in her life. The education, mentoring and support are tools you decide to add to supplement the things that you want to accomplish. You learn and understand that there is no perfect, it doesn't exist. But by choosing to be a work in progress, you are choosing every day to look at the different areas in your life you may be happy with or you may want to improve.

There's nothing wrong with wanting to be better. There's nothing wrong with consistently wanting to work on yourself. No, I don't spend all day every day improving myself. But when I may not react the way that I would prefer in a particular situation, I step back and think, what can I apply from *The Successful Woman's Mindset*? What is it I could've changed? Where could I have improved? That to me is true growth. That to me is what embodies *The Successful Woman's Mindset*.

One of the reasons I believe this book will be a series is because even before I was done writing it and I had my chapters titles, I had already written down another five chapter titles for the next book. As women, we naturally want to improve ourselves. Some of this may be new to you. Some of it you may already be implementing in your life. Some of it could just be a reminder. Reminders are something we need every day and on a consistent basis. Why? Because life happens, we get busy and we forget, and we may react to a situation we would've preferred to react to differently.

As a work in progress, you don't give yourself a hard time about those faltered steps. Instead, you step back, you stop, you are aware, you accept the action that you took, and you look at how you can do it differently next time. What an inspiring world it would be if everybody did that. It may mean even revisiting the situation and making it right. Remember the chapter about accepting your failures and mistakes? We are human after all. And to be human is to err.

I have never met one person who hasn't made a mistake or failed. Not one person who didn't think, "Wait, if I could have a do-over..." Well you know what? You can. That's what being a work in progress is. You may not always have a do-over in the same situation you reacted to. But you can definitely have a do-over for the next time something similar happens. Then, you forgive yourself. Forgiveness is a beautiful thing because when you choose to forgive yourself, that's when true healing happens. We need to learn to forgive others, even if it's just within ourselves, because at times we hold onto the things that others have done. To forgive is to be a work in progress.

What I hope that you get out of this book is this: I, myself, and many successful women I know, are working every day to embrace and master *The Successful Woman's Mindset*. I hope you will take this book, keep it on your nightstand and revisit it often for encouragement and guidance. Remember that the journey to the fulfillment of your dreams is possible when you embrace *The Successful Woman's Mindset*.

ABOUT THE AUTHOR

Galit Ventura-Rozen, M.A. is an award-winning Professional Speaker, Business Performance Expert, creator of The Speakers Method and 25+ year entrepreneur, owning and operating her own Commercial Real Estate Company. Galit has sold over 150 million dollars' worth of income properties such as apartment buildings, office, industrial and retail shopping centers. She works with entrepreneurs and businesses to increase performance, profits, and productivity. She is a well-known professional speaker and corporate trainer on the topics of leadership, effective communication, real estate, business and the successful mindset. She also provides prospective entrepreneurs and professionals the guidance and mentoring to become professional speakers and utilize speaking in their businesses to increase sales by attracting their ideal client. She graduated from University of Nevada with a Bachelor of Science in Business Administration in 1995 and obtained a master's degree in therapy with Honors in 2016. As a serial entrepreneur for over 25 years, Galit has founded many successful and reputable enterprises, as well as acting as a business consultant. Galit is a recipient of the TMG Silver State Award for Best Local Motivational Speaker, a recipient of the National Association of Women Business Owners Southern Nevada Chapter Women of Distinction Award, has been named top 100 women of influence 2 years in a row by MyVegas Magazine, and a Women's Chamber of Commerce of Nevada hall of fame inductee for leadership. Galit serves and has served on multiple philanthropic and professional boards: Women of Global Change, Commercial Real Estate Women, The Shade Tree Women's Shelter, Women's Philanthropy Council and the National Association of Women Business Owners Southern Nevada Chapter. Galit was named The Top 40 Coaches to follow in 2019, People to Watch, and 5 Female Entrepreneurs to get to know. *The Successful Woman's Mindset* is on the list of 100 Top Business Books by Women by Her Business Listings Directory and #10 on Mindfulness Books List.

facebook.com/galitventurarozen
instagram.com/galitventurarozen

You can learn more about Galit at www.galitventurarozen.com.

For more information on programs, workshops, speaking engagements in relation to The Successful Woman's Mindset please visit:

www.thesuccessfulwomansmindset.com.

Make sure to visit www.thesuccessfulwomansmindset.com for your free PDF downloadable workbook to go side by side with this book.

CODE: ACTIVATEYOURPOWER

Made in the USA
Las Vegas, NV
16 February 2021